HOW TO PASS ✓

STANDARD GRADE
GERMAN

Douglas Angus

Hodder Gibson
A MEMBER OF THE HODDER HEADLINE GROUP

Acknowledgements

The Publishers would like to thank the following for permission to reproduce copyright material:

Extracts from the GRC are reprinted by permision of the Scottish Qualifications Authority.

Artworks by Kate Sardella, IFA Design Ltd.

Cartoons © Moira Munro 2005.

CD Acknowledgements

Voices: Jennifer Dieter, Dominik Flury, Michéle Spoerri and Daniel Wiedemann.

Audio Engineering – Phil Booth, Heriot-Watt University.

Every effort has been made to trace all copyright holders, but if any have been inadvertently overlooked the Publishers will be pleased to make the necessary arrangements at the first opportunity.

If the CD is missing from this package, please contact us on 0141 848 1609 or at hoddergibson@hodder.co.uk, advising where and when you purchased the book.

Although every effort has been made to ensure that website addresses are correct at time of going to press, Hodder Gibson cannot be held responsible for the content of any website mentioned in this book. It is sometimes possible to find a relocated web page by typing in the address of the home page for a website in the URL window of your browser.

Papers used in this book are natural, renewable and recyclable products. They are made from wood grown in sustainable forests. The logging and manufacturing processes conform to the environmental regulations of the country of origin.

Orders: please contact Bookpoint Ltd, 130 Milton Park, Abingdon, Oxon OX14 4SB. Telephone: (44) 01235 827720. Fax: (44) 01235 400454. Lines are open from 9.00–6.00, Monday to Saturday, with a 24-hour message answering service. Visit our website at www.hoddereducation.co.uk. Hodder Gibson can be contacted direct on: Tel: 0141 848 1609; Fax: 0141 889 6315; email: hoddergibson@hodder.co.uk

© Douglas Angus 2005
First published in 2005 by
Hodder Gibson, a member of the Hodder Headline Group
2a Christie Street
Paisley PA1 1NB

Impression number	10 9 8 7 6 5 4 3 2 1
Year	2010 2009 2008 2007 2006 2005

All rights reserved. Apart from any use permitted under UK copyright law, no part of this publication may be reproduced or transmitted in any form or by any means, electronic or mechanical, including photocopy, recording, or any information storage and retrieval system, without permission in writing from the publisher or under licence from the Copyright Licensing Agency Limited. Further details of such licences (for reprographic reproduction) may be obtained from the Copyright Licensing Agency Limited, of 90 Tottenham Court Road, London W1T 4LP.

Cover photo © Digital Vision/Getty Images.
Typeset in 10.5 on 14pt Frutiger Light by Phoenix Photosetting, Chatham, Kent
Printed and bound in Great Britain by Arrowsmith, Bristol

A catalogue record for this title is available from the British Library

ISBN-10: 0-340-90609-X

ISBN-13: 978-0-340-90609-5

CONTENTS

Chapter 1	Introduction	1
Chapter 2	Reading	8
Chapter 3	Reading: Foundation and General levels	14
Chapter 4	Reading: Credit level	24
Chapter 5	Answers to the reading questions	31
Chapter 6	Listening	35
Chapter 7	Listening: Foundation and General levels	37
Chapter 8	Listening: Credit level	48
Chapter 9	Transcripts and answers to the listening questions	51
Chapter 10	Speaking	65
Chapter 11	Writing	82
Chapter 12	Structures and vocabulary	90

Chapter 1

INTRODUCTION

This book is a guide to Standard Grade German, to its four skill areas, and to how to get the best possible mark in each area. There are separate sections giving advice on reading, listening, speaking and writing. For reading and listening, there are also practice questions, with answers so that you can check your work. For speaking and writing, we work through some sample questions, looking at how to improve your performance in assessments. The accompanying CD contains listening material, to be used with the questions and transcripts in the book.

What is the exam like?

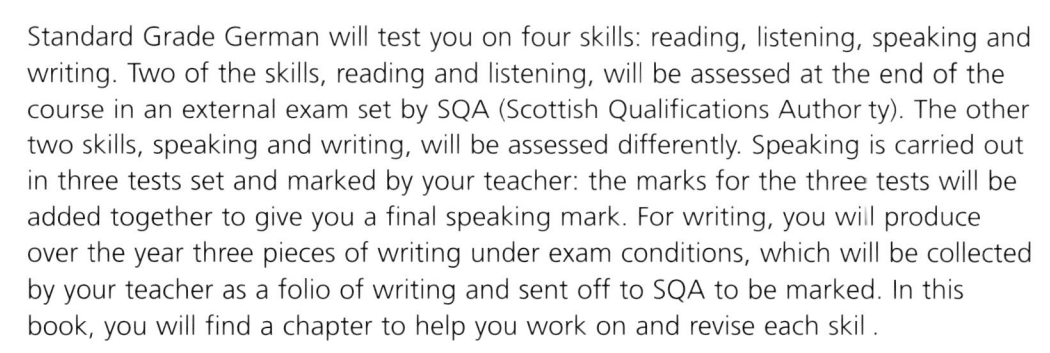

Standard Grade German will test you on four skills: reading, listening, speaking and writing. Two of the skills, reading and listening, will be assessed at the end of the course in an external exam set by SQA (Scottish Qualifications Authority). The other two skills, speaking and writing, will be assessed differently. Speaking is carried out in three tests set and marked by your teacher: the marks for the three tests will be added together to give you a final speaking mark. For writing, you will produce over the year three pieces of writing under exam conditions, which will be collected by your teacher as a folio of writing and sent off to SQA to be marked. In this book, you will find a chapter to help you work on and revise each skill.

How is my final mark made up?

You need to be good at maths to work this one out! You will be given a grade for each of the four skills: speaking and reading will be double weighted in the calculation of your overall award for German. This means:

- **Reading:** the mark you get in the final exam will be doubled.
- **Listening**: the mark you get in the final exam will be added to this.
- **Writing**: the marks you get for your three pieces of writing will be added up, and then divided by three to give a writing grade: this average grade will be added to the listening and reading grades.
- **Speaking**: the marks you get for your three speaking assessments will be added up and divided by three to give you a grade for speaking: this will be doubled and added to the other three grades.
- **Total**: you now have a total mark, which will be divided by six to give you your overall grade.

Chapter 1

What do I have to know?

You will need to know basic vocabulary covering a list of topic areas: see the table on pages 6–7. This will help you listen to and read German more easily. It will also help you produce your own written and spoken German. You will find some useful vocabulary with each of the speaking and writing preparation tasks, as well as with the listening tasks. At the end of the book, there is a list of useful vocabulary broken down by topic area.

You will need to know the basics of grammar, so that you can write and speak German correctly. The basics are in a table on page 5, and there is further work on this area in the speaking and writing chapters.

You must be able to use a dictionary, to help you understand German in the reading exam, and to let you find words you need for your speaking and writing.

What exactly is involved in the exam?

Speaking

Speaking will be assessed by your teacher and externally moderated by SQA. Assessment tasks will arise out of your normal class work.

You will have to carry out three tasks:

- a prepared talk on a topic you choose (using no more than five headings of up to eight words each in English, or in German)
- a conversation (on the same or a different topic)
- a role play requiring polite language (this means you have to use *Sie*, not *du*).

You should be able to demonstrate the ability to take part in a conversation, to use polite language as appropriate and be able to cope with additional questions or problems.

Grades will be awarded for your performance in each of the three types of task. Final grades will be awarded on the basis of the sum of the three grades divided by three. Final grades containing .66 should be rounded up. Final grades containing .33 should be rounded down.

Listening

Listening will be assessed by an external examination. There will be two separate papers, one at each level. You will hear the German three times.

Questions will be set and answered in English, and they may be multiple-choice or gap-filling tasks, even at Credit level.

You will **not** be allowed to use a German–English dictionary.

Reading

Reading will also be assessed by an external examination. There will be two separate papers, one at each level; each paper will include several texts.

Questions will be set and answered in English, including multiple-choice or gap-filling tasks.

Unusual words will be translated for you in a glossary.

At least one passage in each paper will be vocational or work related.

You will be allowed to use a German dictionary.

The reading paper will last 45 minutes at Foundation and General levels and one hour at Credit level.

Writing

Writing will be assessed by means of a folio of three pieces of work which will come from your normal class activities. You may select the topics, or do something your teacher suggests. You can work from headings in either German or English. Your writing can be prepared in advance, drafted and redrafted. The final tests must, however, be produced under controlled conditions: this means that each piece will be written in class, within 30 minutes, under supervision, and you will not be allowed to use notes or refer to a book other than a dictionary.

Pieces of writing should normally be between 25 and 200 words in length, should relate to three different topics or tasks and should be your best work.

All writing tests will be marked externally by SQA.

Basic grammar

When marking your work, teachers will be looking for accuracy in basic structures. This is straightforward, simple language, and you should be able to show you can do at least the following things:

Verbs
- use the correct form of the present tense to express being, having, going, doing, liking and other activities, using regular verb patterns in the first and third persons singular. This includes using subject pronouns (like *ich, er, sie, es*) and correct verb endings, matching the subject
- use negatives like *nicht*, *nie*, etc.
- ask simple questions correctly
- use verbs fairly accurately in personal language and polite language. This includes the correct polite verb forms for requests (*möchten Sie …, ich möchte gern …*) and the correct verb forms for plural subjects (*meine Eltern sind …, meine Freunde haben …*)

- in German, put verbs in their correct place in a sentence: the section on word order in Chapter 12 will help you revise this

Nouns
- use the correct type of article/determiner (*ein/eine, der, die, das*) and, if you can, the correct form (that is, the correct ending: *mein* or *meine*, subject, object or dative)
- use nouns with the correct gender form of article (*der, die* or *das*) and use the correct endings on adjectives
- use the words for 'my' and 'your' correctly.

For better grades, you will have to do more than this: the grammar grid on page 5 shows what markers are going to be looking for. When you are working through the writing and speaking chapters, you should keep referring back to this table, so that you can show off your knowledge of German to the examiner!

Grammar grid for productive language (speaking and writing)

	Foundation	General	Credit
Word order	Shows awareness of different linguistic conventions, e.g. noun/adjective order	Shows some control of different linguistic conventions in straightforward expressions, e.g. position of verbs	Has control of different linguistic conventions in straightforward expressions and shows some control in more complex structures
Person	Can make person understood	Uses subject pronouns/verb endings (as appropriate) fairly consistently and shows awareness of the use of object pronouns	Uses subject and object pronouns consistently and shows awareness of the use of indirect object pronouns
Tense and mood	Can use high-frequency verbs in present tense with some accuracy in first and third persons singular	Can use present tense and at least one other with some accuracy in all persons	Can use a range of tenses as appropriate
	Can articulate basic questions to adults and peers	Can articulate common questions using politeness conventions on more demanding topics and can use common commands	Can ask a range of questions in different ways and can articulate commands
	Can use fixed phrases, e.g. I would like, I must	Can use modal verbs + infinitive in plain and polite forms (e.g. present and conditional)	Can use modal verbs + infinitive in a range of tenses as appropriate
Articles	Uses some form of article/determiner	Uses articles/determiners correctly, but may not be entirely accurate	Uses articles/determiners consistently and accurately
Cases and agreement	Shows awareness of case	Uses correct case with high-frequency expressions	Shows some control of cases (*very important for German*)
	Shows awareness of adjective agreement	Uses correct adjective agreement with high-frequency nouns (regular forms)	Uses correct adjective agreement with a wider range of nouns (regular and some irregular forms)

Chapter 1

How do I go about learning vocabulary?

The best way to revise is to practise, although different people have different ways of learning vocabulary. The following ways might be useful to you:

1. Try writing out a list of words, then reading them out: cover up the German, and see if you can remember it from the English, and of course the other way round.
2. Read things over several times, on different occasions.
3. Check your memorising, either by covering one part and remembering the other, or by getting someone to do it with you (a friend, or a parent). If you have someone who will help you, get them to say a word in English, which you have to put into German.
4. Try to get your words organised into areas, so they all hang together and make sense to you.
5. Use spidergrams of related words.

The topics you will be expected to know about will be the same for all four skills, and the SQA has provided the following list from which to work. These are the areas in which you should know vocabulary to help you cope with the listening tests, where you will not have a dictionary, and also to give you the basic vocabulary for reading tests, so you do not have to keep consulting a dictionary.

Basic topics	Standard Grade topic development
◆ name, age, where you live, nationality, points of the compass, spelling, distances	◆ personal information given/asked for in polite language
◆ members of family, friends, physical description	◆ members of family, friends and friendship, physical and character description, interpersonal problems and relationships
◆ parts of body, illness/accidents	◆ parts of body, illness/accidents, making appointments
◆ own house/rooms	◆ houses/rooms and ideal house
◆ routine	◆ comparison of routine and lifestyles in Scotland and in Germany/German-speaking countries
◆ birthdays, days, dates	◆ life in future, past and future events (in routine)
◆ school subjects, time	◆ comparison of Scottish system with that of German-speaking countries

Chapter 1

INTRODUCTION

- leisure, sports
  - leisure, sports and health issues: healthy eating, exercise, drugs
  - TV, film and music

- foods/drinks
  - other food issues

- snack food
  - restaurants/menus, making arrangements

- simple directions
  - giving simple and complex directions

- buildings
  - tourist information, comparison of town/country, helping the environment

- pocket money
  - changing money

- simple transactions, e.g. souvenirs, gifts, clothes, accommodation, snacks, transport
  - dealing with problems in transactions

- jobs/working and studying
  - relative merits of jobs
  - work experience
  - future employment

- countries/place
  - travel information
  - travel plans
  - relative merits of different means of transport
  - comparisons between different countries

- weather
  - weather

- holidays
  - future holidays
  - ideal holidays
  - past holidays

Chapter 2

READING

Reading is worth **one-third** of your overall Standard Grade result: it will be tested in an external exam. The test at Foundation and General levels will last 45 minutes, and at Credit level will last 60 minutes. You will be allowed to use a dictionary for this exam, so you need to be very confident about your dictionary use. Most dictionaries contain a guide to using the dictionary: make sure you look at this before you start answering questions, especially if you ever find a dictionary annoying!

The key to this assessment is finding the correct answer, and missing out the bits you do not need. Reading is a skill, and a skill you need to work on to allow you to give of your best in the final exam. The way to succeed is to extract from the text what you actually need for your answers, and to ignore the rest: the exam will test your ability to extract relevant information from the text. That means there is a lot of material which is irrelevant, and which you do not need. The skill you have to develop is the skill of identifying which bits you actually need.

There is a suggested sequence for you to follow:

1. Read the information in English about the text at the start: this should give you clues as to what the answers are going to be about. Keep this information in your head as you answer the questions!
2. Now look at the questions: this should tell you where to look in the passage for your answers. Look for clue words in the question which will show you where the answer is to be found.
3. Only now should you look at the text: skim through it to get an idea of what it is about, without using a dictionary!
4. Now look for the key areas which match your questions, and start looking for the answers just there. Remember the questions will follow the same order as the text, and you should not have to jump around all over the place.

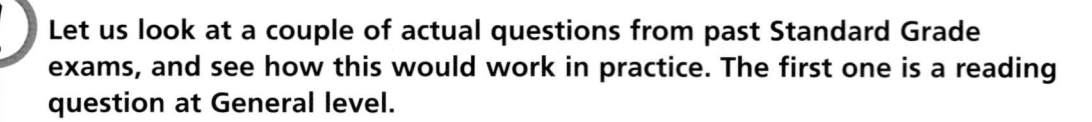

Let us look at a couple of actual questions from past Standard Grade exams, and see how this would work in practice. The first one is a reading question at General level.

Chapter 2

In a magazine, you read about a German girl, Katrin Wypior, who is 'Personality of the month'

Katrin Wypior

Ich bin fünfzehn und spiele seit fünf Jahren Geige. Mein Haupt-hobby ist aber Lesen. Klassische Musik höre ich nie. Ich höre lieber Gruppen wie 911. Mein Traum ist es, eine Weltreise zu machen.

Mein größter Fehler ist wahrscheinlich, dass ich sehr faul bin. Was ich an mir besonders mag: ich komme prima mit meinen Freunden aus.

Your task is to complete the grid below.

Name	Katrin Wypior
Age	15
Main hobby	
Favourite music	Groups like 911
Her dream	
Worst fault	
Best quality	

1 From the grid, you should know what you are looking for.

2 The first box you are asked to fill in is her hobby: look for this word in the text, and you will find it in *Haupthobby*. German is very helpful sometimes, because all nouns have capitals: you are looking for a noun here, as it is a hobby, and you will find the word is *Lesen*. If you are not sure of the word, look it up and you will find the verb *lesen*, which means 'read'. This should give you the answer: **reading**.

3 The next box looks for her dream: you can either recognise *Traum* as 'dream', or use the dictionary in a reverse way, which often saves a lot of time. Look up 'dream' and you will find *Traum*: this shows you where in the text to find your

9

answer. Her dream is a *Weltreise*. Remember that German loves to join words together to make new words, and you may have to break down a word to get its parts: in this case you get 'world' and 'trip', which should allow you to work out a **trip around the world**.

4   You are asked to find her worst fault: again, reverse use of the dictionary gives you *Fehler*. What is her *Fehler*? She is *faul*. If you don't know the word, look it up and you will find that it means **lazy**.

5   For the last answer, you know where to look, as the answers all come in order. If you are not sure what this sentence means, look for the verbs: the verbs are always the key to the meaning of a sentence. You should know that verbs come second and last in a clause or sentence, so you get *mag* ('like'), *komme* and *aus*. Look up *komme ... aus* as one word, *auskomme*, and you should find 'get on with'. In the same sentence, you will find *Freunden*, so the answer must be that **she gets on with her friends**. It is really important for reading that you can identify the verbs: if you find this difficult, look in Chapter 12 at the sections on verbs and tenses.

The next example is from a Credit paper.

Two girls, Natalie and Isabella, tell us about their hobbies and why they chose them

Natalie's hobby is playing the saxophone

Geige- und Klavier-spielen sagen mir nichts. Saxophon ist viel außergewöhnlicher. Außerdem gibt's nicht viele, die das machen. Ich habe mich in mein Sax von Anfang an verliebt. Zwar braucht man viel Luft, aber man bekommt sofort einen Ton raus. Wenn ich Jazz oder Blues spiele, kann ich kreativ sein.

Isabella's hobby is photography

Menschen haben mich total fasziniert, daher habe ich so gern fotografiert. Man kann Menschen von einer Seite zeigen, die man sonst vielleicht nicht sieht. Daher habe ich in New York die Menschen fotografiert und eben nicht das Empire State Building.

Jetzt weiß ich einigermaßen über die Technik Bescheid. Als Folge habe ich mehr Interesse an Schulfächern wie Chemie und Physik.

(a) What appeals to Natalie about playing the saxophone? Write **three** things. **3**

(b) What attracts Isabella to photography? Write **two** things. **2**

(c) How has Isabella's hobby helped her at school? **1**

1. By looking at question (a), you should notice that you are being asked about Natalie's opinions: why she likes playing the saxophone. You will find opinion words in Chapter 12; but you should also search the text for adjectives, describing words, as well as for verbs. The magic words here are *außergewöhnlicher* ('unusual') and *kreativ*. *Kreativ* is linked with *spiele*: this should enable you to work out that **she finds playing the saxophone creative** when playing jazz and blues, and that she likes it because **it is unusual**. For your third mark, you will find *bekommt* (which means 'gets') and *Ton* (which means 'sound'): **you get a sound straightaway**.

2. For question (b), you should look at the start of the paragraph, as it has the word *gern*, showing you that is where her opinion is. Look at the verb *fasziniert*: 'fascinated'. Your first answer is: **she is fascinated by people** (*Menschen*). Carry on: the verbs are *kann ... zeigen* ('can show') and *nicht sieht* ('don't see'). **You can show people from a side you don't otherwise see.**

3. To answer question (c), look for 'school': when you find it, you will also find two subjects and the word *Interesse*. **She is more interested in Chemistry and Physics.**

Chapter 2

> **Remember, only look up what you have to: know where to look for the answer, and know what you are looking for. Verbs and nouns are the two most important things!**

The other major skill needed for reading exams is using a dictionary: it is very easy to spend far too long looking up words, and also very easy to find the wrong answer. What is worse, sometimes you cannot find any answer! It is usual to blame the dictionary for this, but more often than not it is the person using the dictionary who has got it wrong! Make sure you know your alphabet properly, and practise using the dictionary. When you do use it, remember the following things:

- When you find a word, the next thing after it in many dictionaries is often the guide to pronouncing it! It might also be a word like *pret.* or *p.t.*, which is the dictionary's way of telling you the word you are looking up is a past tense, or *prep.*, which tells you it is a preposition.
- There will often be several entries for a word, because some words are both verb and noun, with different meanings.
- Because German verbs have endings, you will often not find exactly the word you are looking for: you need the infinitive.
- Don't just look at the start of the entry, go on down the entry to see if something further down makes sense.
- Always keep in mind the context of the passage you are reading: that may well help you to find the correct phrase in a dictionary.
- Watch for the little bracketed words in some dictionaries, like *(sport)*, which tell you what context the word is used in.
- Remember: sometimes it makes sense to look up words in the English half of the dictionary, to give you a clue as to where to look for the answer to a question.

> **If the answer asks for two things, just give two things! The examiner will only give you marks for the first two things you write down, and you will get no credit for something you get right later on in the answer if there is a wrong answer given before it.**

Vocabulary tips

There are some vocabulary areas which always come up in the exam, and it is important that you know and are able to recognise these words, as it will save time with the dictionary in the exam:

- numbers, including times, dates, temperatures, distances and prices
- days, months, weeks and years

Chapter 2

- jobs and professions
- school, including subjects
- food and drink
- family members
- the weather
- hobbies and sports
- daily routine and household tasks
- places in town
- methods of transport
- houses and rooms in the house
- question words and phrases.

READING

Chapter 3

READING: FOUNDATION AND GENERAL LEVELS

1 You read this information about travel in Germany

In the summer, you are going to make your own way to Germany to stay with a friend of your family in Bergisch Gladbach. The family send you some information they think might be useful.

Tickets aus dem Internet!

Jetzt können Reisende ihre Fahrscheine im Internet nicht nur bestellen, sondern auch am eigenen Computer ausdrucken. Die Deutsche Bahn hat diesen „Surf & Rail" Service für Verbindungen zwischen 25 deutschen Städten. Kunden können für diese Reisen Karten zu Sonderpreisen kaufen.

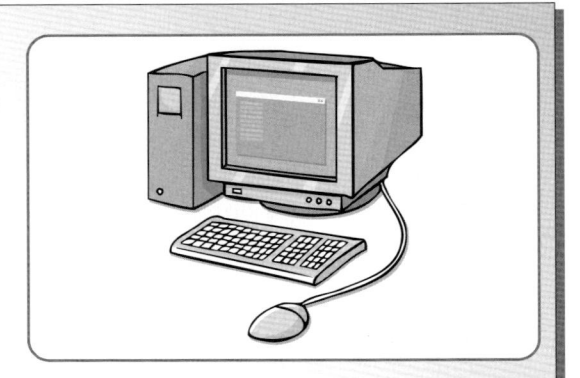

Man bezahlt mit der Kreditkarte. Eine Hin- und Rückfahrt von Berlin nach Köln mit „Surf & Rail" kostet 75 Euro. Der Normalpreis ist aber 195 Euro.

Tick the correct box for each of these statements. 5

	True	False
You can order your ticket on the Internet		
You can print the ticket on your own computer		
You can buy tickets for anywhere in Europe		
Tickets cost a little more this way		
You can pay with a credit card		

2 You read this article about a well-known star who comes from Bergisch Gladbach

Topmodel Heidi kommt aus Bergisch Gladbach!

Ein perfekter Körper ist ihr Kapital. Heidi wollte gar nicht Model werden, sondern Designerin, als 1991 die Frauenzeitschrift „Petra" einen Wettbewerb hatte – und die beste Freundin überredete Schülerin Heidi. Sie machte mit. Nach fünf Monaten Warten kam dann der Durchbruch: Siegerin bei der Zeitschrift „Petra" und ein Vertrag bei der Agentur „Metropolitan".

Add in the missing word or words: 5

Heidi originally wanted to become a ....

Petra is a ....

.... persuaded Heidi to take part in the competition.

At the time, she was a ....

When she won, she also received a ....

3 You read this tourist leaflet about Bergisch Gladbach

While you are in Bergisch Gladbach, the family plan to have a big party for you. They send you this leaflet from the tourist office telling you where they plan to have it.

Feiern mit einer Grillparty

Wer sein Grillwürstchen gerne mit ein bisschen Waldluft isst, der liegt mit einer der Bergisch Gladbacher Grillhütten genau richtig: im Park Diepeschrath sind sie zu finden. Mit viel Platz für große Gruppen, allem Komfort wie Strom und Toiletten sind diese Hütten einfach ideal für Geburtstage und Hochzeiten. Buchen Sie frühzeitig, die Grillhütten sind heiß begehrt!

(a) What kind of party are they planning to have for you?   1

....

(b) Where will they have this?   1

....

(c) What facilities are on hand?   2

....

(d) Because they are popular, what must you do?   1

....

4 You read an article about the German singles charts

Die Hitparade

Wechsel an der Spitze der deutschen Single-Charts: nach zehn Wochen ist „Schnappi, das kleine Krokodil" nicht mehr auf Platz 1. Popsängerin Nena verdrängte sie mit „Liebe ist".

(a) How long was 'Schnappi' number one in the charts?   1

....

(b) What was the name of the singer who replaced it?   1

....

5 You read this article about children's 'invisible friends'

Der unsichtbare Freund

Der imaginäre Freund von Kindern im Alter zwischen zwei und vier Jahren muss nicht für Eltern ein Problem sein. Es ist im Vorschulalter ganz normal. Eltern sollten den imaginären Freund von den Kindern akzeptieren. Junge Leute, die in ihrer Kindheit einen unsichtbaren Freund hatten, finden es später leichter, Freunde zu machen.

Complete the sentences below.

(a) Children often have imaginary friends between the ages of .... and **2**

(b) Parents should **1**

(c) Children who have had an imaginary friend find **1**

....

6 You read this article about paying for goods in a supermarket

Fingerabdruck ersetzt Kreditkarte

Einkaufen per Fingerabdruck – ohne Bargeld und Kreditkarte: das erprobt der Supermarkt Edeka Südwest. Edeka ist der weltweit erste Lebensmittelhändler, der dieses neue Bezahlsystem probiert.

Der Kunde muss nach dem Einkauf an der Kasse seinen Finger auf einen Scanner legen, um die Waren zu erhalten. Edeka bekommt das Geld dann direkt bei seiner Bank.

Are the following statements **true** or **false**? Write **T** or **F** in the boxes below.   3

You need both a credit card and your fingerprint	
Edeka is the first company in the world to introduce the system	
The money is taken direct from your bank account	

7 You read in a school newspaper what two young people think about working in part-time jobs and going to school at the same time

Jobben auf der Schule

Klaus: Ich besuche die 11. Klasse eines Gymnasiums und habe keinen Job. Ich glaube, dass es für Schüler nicht immer eine gute Idee ist, wenn sie in ihrer Freizeit viel arbeiten. Das kann zu Problemen mit den Hausaufgaben führen.

Karin: Seit einem halben Jahr arbeite ich um mir noch was zu sparen. Danach gehe ich weiter zur Schule. Ich finde, dass man auch arbeiten kann, wenn man zur Schule geht. Man soll nicht seinen Eltern um Geld bitten müssen. Zeitungen austragen oder im Supermarkt arbeiten finde ich okay. Das kann bis zu 200 Euro im Monat einbringen.

(a) Does Klaus have a part-time job?   1

....

(b) What does he think the dangers of part-time jobs are?   1

....

(c) How long has Karin been working?   1

....

(d) Why does she work?   1

....

(e) What **two** jobs does she think are all right for pupils?   2

....

....

8 You read this interview with the German film actress Franka Potente, who has returned to Germany from the USA

Franka Potente

Letztes Jahr kam die 30-jährige Filmschauspielerin Franka Potente nach zwei Jahren in Los Angeles wieder nach Berlin. Sie suchte Heimat, alte Freunde und gute Gespräche.

Warum hast du L.A. verlassen?
Weil ich einfach wieder Lust hatte, nach Hause zu gehen. Dorthin, wo Arbeit ist und meine Freunde sind. Ich bin Europäerin.

(a) How long was she in America?   1

....

(b) Mention any **two** things that brought her back.   2

....

Chapter 3

9 Now read the rest of the interview, in which Franka talks about the recent role she had in a film

Regisseur Christopher Smith hat dir die Hauptrolle in dem britischen Horrorfilm „Creep" gegeben. Wie fühlte sich die Rolle der Kate an?

Wir haben in London in einer alten U-Bahn-Station gedreht. Jeden Morgen sind wir um sechs Uhr 800 Stufen ins Dunkle gelaufen. Es war kalt, und zugig. Das war schon sehr unheimlich. Und ich finde auch dieses britische „running lunch" ein Problem: man serviert das Essen auf Papptellern und du musst es dann ganz schnell essen.

(a) Where did they make the film? Mention **two** things.   2

....

(b) What were the conditions like? Mention **two** things.   2

....

(c) What did she not like about the catering? Mention **two** things.   2

....

10 You read this article about some German pupils involved in enterprise education

Schülerinnen gründen Firma

Es ist Mittwoch, fünfzehn Uhr in der Cafeteria der Maria-Wart-Schule in Landau. Normalerweise ist um diese Uhrzeit niemand hier auf der Schule, heute ist die ganze Klasse hier. Die „Mitarbeiterinnen" der Schülerfirma „Calendrix" produzieren gerade ihren neuen Kalender. Die Schülerinnen nehmen mit ihrer Firma „Calendrix" am Projekt „JUNIOR – Schule als Manager" teil.

(a) What day and time is it?   2

....

(b) What is unusual about today?   2

....

(c) What are they producing for their project?   1

....

11 You come across this article about a German exchange student

Fastfood und Dresscode

Erfahrungen einer Austauschschülerin in den USA

Andrea (sechzehn) kommt aus Stuttgart und ist seit Juli 2005 Gastschülerin an der „Sunnyside Highschool" im Bundesstaat Washington, USA. Sie wohnt für elf Monate bei einer amerikanischen Familie, wo sie eine „neue" Mutter und „neue" Geschwister im Alter von zwölf und achtzehn Jahren hat.

(a) How long will she stay in the USA?   1

....

(b) What are we told about the family she is staying with?   2

....

12 You carry on reading the article: she is asked about feeling homesick

Hast du Heimweh?

Nein, Heimweh habe ich kaum, denn es gefällt mir hier sehr gut. Vieles ist aber anders als in Deutschland. Zum Beispiel gibt es hier keine öffentlichen Verkehrsmittel, auch das ungesunde Essen ist sehr schlecht. Positiv ist aber, dass Autofahren bereits ab sechzehn Jahren erlaubt ist.

(a) How does she feel about where she is staying?   1

....

(b) Give one positive and one negative thing she mentions.   2

positive	
negative	

13 She is asked about how she keeps in contact with home

Wie oft hast du Kontakt zu deiner Familie und zu deinen Freunden?

Mit meinen Eltern telefoniere ich drei bis vier Mal im Monat; außerdem schreibe ich ihnen E-Mails. Zu meinen Großeltern und meinen Freunden habe ich ebenfalls ab und zu Telefonkontakt; auch ihnen schreibe ich regelmäßig Mails.

(a) How does she keep in touch with her parents? Write **two** things.   **2**

....

(b) Who else does she keep in touch with?   **2**

....

14 You find an article in which some young people are asked how they see their future

Wo siehst du dich in zehn Jahren?

Wir haben fünf junge Menschen gefragt:

Raphaela
Mit Ende zwanzig möchte ich mit dem Mann meines Lebens wohnen und meinen Traumberuf gefunden haben.

Axel
In zehn Jahren werde ich auf dem Land wohnen. Ich werde eine Familie haben, einige Kinder, und meine Frau wird sich auch in der Arbeit engagieren.

Alexander
In zehn Jahren habe ich sicher einen Job. Ich würde gerne meine eigene Firma haben und Autos verkaufen. Ich werde mich auf Offroadfahrzeuge spezialisieren.

Jasmin
In zehn Jahren will ich eine Weltreise gemacht haben und mit dem Studium fertig sein. Wenn ich dann selbstständig bin, werde ich auch eine Familie gründen, vielleicht im Ausland.

Melanie
In zehn Jahren möchte ich selbst-ständig sein und fest im Leben stehen. Ich liebe aber meine Familie. Deshalb werde ich auch hier bleiben.

Match the names to the statements below.   5

	would like to have his own company
	might live abroad
	would not want to move away
	would like to live in the country
	would like to have her dream job

Chapter 4

READING: CREDIT LEVEL

1 You read this advice in a magazine for young people in Germany who are about to leave school

Hurra, die Schule ist aus!

Warum Gedanken über die Zeit nach der Schule eine gute Idee sind.

Was soll ich machen, wenn ich die Schule verlasse? Die vielfältigen Chancen, die Schulabgänger heute haben, machen eine Entscheidung nicht gerade einfach. Uni? Berufsschule? Direkt an eine Lehrstelle? Wo also anfangen? Am besten fragst du dich, welche beruflichen Wünsche du hast und – ganz ehrlich – welche Fähigkeiten du in dir hast. Um das herauszufinden, kannst du ein Berufsinteressentest durchmachen.

(a) What **three** choices are mentioned for a young person leaving school? 3

....

....

....

(b) What **two** questions should you ask yourself? 2

....

....

Es gibt viele Berufstests von verschiedenen Anbietern, und manchmal musst du auch für solche Tests zahlen. Es gibt aber diesen Berufsinteressentest, „Du und die Arbeit", kostenlos bei der Agentur für Arbeit.

„Wichtig ist, dass die Fragen nicht eindeutig auf bestimmte Berufe zielen, sonst kann der Test sehr leicht zu falschen Ergebnissen führen", erklärt Martin Lehmann, Berufsberater in der Agentur für Arbeit. Die Testergebnisse hängen auch oft vom Selbstbild der Testperson ab. Kennst du dich gut? Nur wenn du deine Schwächen und Stärken gut einschätzen kannst, profitierst du von dem Test.

(c) What is special about the test *Du und die Arbeit*?   1

....

(d) What must you know to make proper use of this test?   2

....

2 You read this article about the damage caused by parents not being strict enough when bringing up their children

Milde Erziehungsmethoden schaden Kindern

Zu wenig Disziplin hilft unseren Kindern nicht. Viele Eltern sind aber bei der Erziehung ihrer Kinder zu *nachsichtig. Sie versuchen das Leben ihrer Kinder perfekt zu gestalten und sie vor allen Gefahren zu beschützen. Dr. Dan Kindlon führte eine Studie an 700 Teenagern im Alter von vier bis neunzehn Jahren und 1 100 Elternpaaren durch. Er analysierte die Kinder und die Regeln im Haushalt. Die Eltern vieler Kinder sind nicht streng, wenn es um's Fluchen geht, welche Filme die Kinder sehen und welche Videospiele sie spielen. Ein weiteres Charakteristikum ist, dass die Familien nicht gemeinsam essen.

*nachsichtig – *lenient, soft*

(a) What are the parents trying to do, when being lenient?   2

....

....

(b) Which **three** areas are mentioned where parents are not strict enough?   3

....

....

....

Nur zwölf Prozent der untersuchten Kinder leben in Familien, in denen fixe Regeln, Limits und Disziplin herrschen. Diese Kinder nehmen keine Drogen, sind weder aggressiv oder faul, noch unruhig oder depressiv. Ein zentrales Ritual dieser Familien ist das gemeinsame Essen, die Kinder müssen im Haushalt helfen und ihr Zimmer aufräumen.

(c) In households where there is more discipline, how are the children? Mention any **three** things.   **3**

....

....

....

(d) What **three** things are common to these households?   **3**

....

....

....

> Warum sind so viele Eltern so nachsichtig? Meistens arbeiten beide Mutter und Vater und sie kompensieren Schuldgefühle durch materielle Dinge. Oft sind die Eltern auch einfach zu müde um Regeln und Ordnungen durchzusetzen. Darüber hinaus sehen die Eltern ihre Kinder oft als sehr wichtig in ihrem Leben, also wollen sie nicht zu oft „Nein" zu ihren Kindern sagen.

(e) What reasons does the author give for parents being lenient?   **3**

....

....

....

(f) Why don't parents like saying 'no' to their children?   **1**

....

Chapter 4

3 You read this article about how the German tourist industry is trying to help people with mobility problems to travel

Mit Handicap in Urlaub

Der Reisemarkt für Urlauber mit Handicap wird immer größer, und bald wird ein neues Programm diesen Touristen eine barrierefreie Reisewelt anbieten. Unter dem Titel „Reisen für Alle" werden auf der Internationalen Tourismusbörse Berlin neue Möglichkeiten für immobile Reisende gezeigt. Vor allem profitieren Gehbehinderte, Reisende mit Kinderwagen und kleinen Kindern, und Kranke oder Menschen mit Sportverletzungen. „Es handelt sich bei diesem Angebot nicht nur um reine Behindertenreisen – die Arrangements sind auch für Familien und *Senioren, also ältere Reisende, und Urlauber mit schwerem Gepäck geeignet", sagt Projektorganisatorin Friederike Hansen.

*Senioren – *senior citizens, the elderly*

(a) Name **three** groups of people the programme aims to help.   3

....

....

....

(b) Which other groups of people will also be helped?   3

....

....

....

Viele Studien zeigen, dass „Reisen für Alle" ein großer, aber oft unterschätzter Markt sind. Schon jetzt erzielt der barrierefreie Tourismus einen Nettoumsatz von 2,5 Mrd. Euro und sichert damit 65 000 Arbeitsplätze.

Die Touristikindustrie denkt auch an den Seniorenmarkt. Es gibt einen Trend, dass immer mehr Großeltern auch außerhalb der Hochsaison mit den Enkeln verreisen. Für die Industrie ist der Seniorenmarkt ein wichtiges Marktsegment, denn der Gesamtanteil der Seniorinnen und Senioren an der Bevölkerung wächst rapide. Im Jahr 2010 wird jeder vierte Deutsche über 60 Jahre alt sein, 2030 sogar jeder Dritte.

(c) What trend has the tourist industry noticed recently? **2**

....

(d) What information are we given about 'senior citizens' in Germany? **3**

....

....

4 You come across this advice for parents for dealing with hay fever sufferers

Heuschnupfen: wie Eltern ihren Kindern helfen können

Mit dem Frühling kommt auch wieder das Kribbeln in der Nase: der Heuschnupfen ist wieder da. In Deutschland ist bereits jedes sechste Kind von dieser Reaktion des Immunsystems betroffen. Der schöne Nachmittag der Kinder zwischen Blumen und Gras bringt dann Symptome, besonders in der Hochsaison von März bis Oktober, wie heftige Niesanfällen, juckende und brennende Augen und eine Schnupfnase. In den Apotheken findet man verschiedene Medikamente bereit, die mit den schlimmsten Symptomen helfen können.

(a) How many children in Germany suffer from hay fever? **1**

....

(b) Which three symptoms are mentioned? **3**

....

(c) What is the first solution offered? **1**

....

Aber auch einige einfache Schritte können während der Pollen-Hochsaison im Kampf gegen den Heuschnupfen nützlich sein.
- ❏ Die Pollenbelastung im Sommer ist oder nach Regenschauern nicht so groß.
- ❏ Nicht vergessen, die Wohnung zu durchlüften.
- ❏ Um die Mittagszeit sind die Pollen auch rar.
- ❏ Eltern sollen die getragene Kleidung der Kinder nicht im Kinderzimmer lassen, so können sich keine Pollen in der Kleidung festsetzten.
- ❏ Es bringt den Kindern Entlastung, wenn sie sich vor dem Zubettgehen die Haare waschen. Auf diese Weise kann das Kind besser schlafen.
- ❏ Im Urlaub sind Orte in den Bergen und am Meer fast pollenfreie Zonen.

(d) Complete the box below: 6

The pollen count is lower	
Don't forget to	
Pollen is not so common at	
Parents shouldn't allow	
Before going to bed, children should	
On holiday, choose areas such as	

5 In the same magazine you read advice for asthma sufferers

Tipps für Asthma-Kranke

Bei Asthmatikern spielen die Behandlung durch den Arzt und das Vermeiden von *Allergie-Auslösern eine zentrale Rolle. Hier geben wir Tipps und Tricks, wie sich das Asthma-Risiko im Haushalt vermeiden lässt.

Auf dem ersten Platz der To-do-Liste steht das Rauchen. Zigarettenkonsum aufgeben schont die schwachen Lungen und verhindert, dass Schadstoffe permanent in der Wohnung sind.

*Auslöser – *trigger, cause*

(a) What **two** things play a central role in dealing with asthma? 2

....

....

(b) Which **two** reasons for stopping smoking are mentioned? 2

....

....

Chapter 4

> Eine weitere Gefahrenquelle stellt das Kinderschlafzimmer dar. Kopfkissen und Bettdecke sollten bei Asthma-Erkrankten keine Vogelfedern enthalten und einmal in der Woche frisch sein. Das Waschen bei mindestens 50 Grad Celsius hilft auch. Auf dem Boden sollten keine Teppiche liegen, damit sich der Staub nicht festsetzen kann. Empfehlenswert ist ein Boden aus Holz oder Fliesen, denn er kann regelmäßig einfach gereinigt werden. Weitere Staubfänger wie Möbel, Heizungen usw. sollten einmal wöchentlich gründlich abgestaubt werden. Auch Zimmerpflanzen sind häufig Allergen-Ursache.

(c) What **two** things should be done about bedding?   **2**

....

....

(d) What advice are we given about flooring?   **4**

....

....

(e) What other sources of dust are mentioned? Give any **two**.   **2**

....

....

Chapter 5

ANSWERS TO THE READING QUESTIONS

Foundation and General levels

1 **Tickets aus dem Internet!**

	True	False
You can order your ticket on the Internet	✓	
You can print the ticket on your own computer	✓	
You can buy tickets for anywhere in Europe		✓
Tickets cost a little more this way		✓
You can pay with a credit card	✓	

2 **Topmodel Heidi kommt aus Bergisch Gladbach!**

Heidi originally wanted to become a **fashion designer**.

Petra is a **(women's) magazine**.

Her best friend persuaded Heidi to take part in the competition.

At the time, she was a **schoolgirl**.

When she won, she also received a **contract (with an agency)**.

3 **Feiern mit einer Grillparty**
   (a) **a barbecue**
   (b) **at the barbecue huts, in the park, at Diepeschrath** (any one)
   (c) **room for groups, electricity, toilets** (any two)
   (d) **book early**

4 **Die Hitparade**
   (a) **ten weeks**
   (b) **Nena**

5 **Der unsichtbare Freund**
   (a) Children often have imaginary friends between the ages of **two** and **four**.
   (b) Parents should **accept the friend/not see it as a problem**.
   (c) Children who have had an imaginary friend find **it easier to make friends later**.

6 **Fingerabdruck ersetzt Kreditkarte**

You need both a credit card and your fingerprint	F
Edeka is the first company in the world to introduce the system	T
The money is taken direct from your bank account	T

7 **Jobben auf der Schule**
   (a) **no**
   (b) **problems with homework**
   (c) **for six months/half a year**
   (d) **to save money, to avoid having to ask parents for money** (any one)
   (e) **delivering newspapers, working in a supermarket**

8 **Franka Potente's return to Germany**
   (a) **two years**
   (b) **home, old friends, good conversations** (any two)

9 **Franka Potente's role in a film**
   (a) **in London, in an (old) underground station**
   (b) **cold, draughty, spooky** (any two)
   (c) **food on paper plates, had to eat fast**

10 **Schülerinnen gründen Firma**
   (a) **Wednesday, 3p.m.**
   (b) **normally no one in school at this time, whole class is here**
   (c) **a calendar**

11 **Fastfood und Dresscode**
   (a) **eleven months**
   (b) **mother, two other children (aged twelve and eighteen)** (lose a mark if you gave the answer 'two sisters')

12 **Hast du Heimweh?**
   (a) **she likes it very much or she finds it very different**
   (b)

positive	Can drive a car from age sixteen
negative	No public transport, food is unhealthy (bad)

13 Wie oft hast du Kontakt zu deiner Familie und zu deinen Freunden?

(a) **phones three or four times a month, writes e-mails**

(b) **grandparents, friends**

14 Wo siehst du dich in zehn Jahren?

Alexander	would like to have his own company
Jasmin	might live abroad
Melanie	would not want to move away
Axel	would like to live in the country
Raphaela	would like to have her dream job

Credit level

1. Hurra, die Schule ist aus!
   (a) **university, further education college, an apprenticeship**
   (b) **what are your job wishes, what abilities (strengths) do you have?**
   (c) **it is free**
   (d) **yourself, your strengths, your weaknesses** (any two)

2. Milde Erziehungsmethoden schaden Kindern
   (a) **make their children's life perfect, protect them from danger**
   (b) **swearing, which films they watch, which videogames they play**
   (c) **don't take drugs, are not aggressive, lazy, restless, depressed** (any three)
   (d) **have meals together, children help in house, tidy their rooms**
   (e) **parents both work and feel guilty, compensate with material things, too tired to impose order**
   (f) **their children are very important to them**

3. Mit Handicap in Urlaub
   (a) **those with difficulty walking, travellers with young children or prams, ill or injured people**
   (b) **old people, those with heavy luggage, families**
   (c) **more and more grandparents/are taking grandchildren on holidays (out of high season)**
   (d) **their numbers are growing rapidly/in 2010 one in four/in 2030 one in three will be over sixty**

Chapter 5

4 **Heuschnupfen: wie Eltern ihren Kindern helfen können**
   (a) **one in six**
   (b) **sneezing, itchy (burning) eyes, a runny nose**
   (c) **medicine from the chemist**
   (d)

The pollen count is lower	in summer, after a rainshower (any one)
Don't forget to	air the flat
Pollen is not so common at	midday
Parents shouldn't allow	clothes they have been wearing outdoors in the children's rooms
Before going to bed, children should	wash their hair
On holiday, choose areas such as	mountains or the sea

5 **Tipps für Asthma-Kranke**
   (a) **treatment by doctor, avoiding triggers for asthma**
   (b) **spares the lungs, keeps toxic substances out of flat**
   (c) **make sure there are no feathers in pillows or quilt/bedspread, change them once a week, wash them at at least 50 degrees** (any two)
   (d) **avoid carpets, as the dust will stay in them, use wood or tiles, as they can be cleared of dust once a week**
   (e) **furniture, radiators, house plants** (any two)

Chapter 6

LISTENING

Listening is worth **one-sixth** of your overall Standard Grade result: it will be tested in an external exam, and the test at each level will last about 20 to 25 minutes. You will not be able to use a dictionary for this exam, so you need to be prepared for it in advance, and make sure you know the basic vocabulary which comes up again and again.

To help with your revision, the listening passages in this guide are broken into topic areas: in the real exam, there will be a variety of topic areas covered within each paper.

The key to this exam is concentration, as the questions come at set intervals, and you cannot ask to hear them again if you were not paying attention! The German on which your questions will be based is repeated three times, with a gap of a few seconds between each passage. For Foundation and General questions, there is always a 30 second gap between each separate passage, and at Credit level this gap is usually 40 seconds. If you get your question answered very quickly, then it is easy to lose concentration while waiting for the next passage: try to prepare for the next question by reading it in advance, so that when you hear the German, you are focused and know what you are listening out for.

Try not to write anything down during the first listening, even if you know the answer: you will have plenty of time later. It is very tempting to dash things down, so that you don't forget them, but realistically that is not going to happen! You also risk missing out important details, because you are concentrating on writing. Use that first listening to make sure you hear everything, and to give you a guide for which bit you have to listen to extra carefully for details you are required to give in your answer.

Make sure you know what you are listening for: particularly at the end of the General paper and in the Credit paper there will be lots of information you don't need, which just acts as interference when you are listening. Focus on what is needed for the answer.

If you are not sure of an answer, go ahead and guess, as what you guess will be a secret between the examiner and you! However, try to make it an intelligent guess: if what you have written looks daft to you, then it probably is: your answer should make sense.

Chapter 6

> If the answer asks for two things, just give two things! The examiner will only give you marks for the first two things you write down, and you will get no credit for something you get right later on in the answer if there is a wrong answer given before it.

Vocabulary tips

There are some vocabulary areas which always come up in the listening exam, and it is important that you know and are able to recognise these words, as you do not have a dictionary in the exam. These vocabulary areas are:

- numbers, including times, dates, temperatures, distances and prices
- days, months, weeks and years
- jobs and professions
- school, including subjects
- food and drink
- family members
- the weather
- hobbies and sports
- daily routine and household tasks
- places in town
- methods of transport
- houses and rooms in the house
- question words and phrases.

> Each question from the listening tests in this book has been recorded as a separate track on the accompanying CD, to help you to easily find the parts that you want to practise.
>
> The track numbers are given in brackets after the questions, for example, (*12*).
>
> The marks available are given in bold, for example, **3**.

Chapter 7

LISTENING: FOUNDATION AND GENERAL LEVELS

1 Questions about school

You will hear a series of questions related to school: before you listen, revise the days of the week, school subjects, and times. Anything else you have learned on this topic is also worth looking over.

1 At what time does Thorsten's school day start and finish? When does he have a break, and for how long? *(2)* **4**

start	
finish	
break starts	
length of break	

2 Which days does he go to school? Tick each day he is at school. Which is his favourite day? Which day does he not like? Mark them with a tick. *(3)* **3**

	school?	favourite	not so good!
Monday			
Tuesday			
Wednesday			
Thursday			
Friday			
Saturday			

3 At what time does he have to get up for school? How does he get to school? *(4)* **2**

He gets up at .... and goes to school by ....

4 How long has he been at his present school? Which class is he in? *(5)* **2**

He has been there for .... He is in the .... class.

5 When do classes start on Wednesday afternoon? *(6)* **1**

Classes start at ....

Chapter 7

6 Why does he mention Herr Fitsch? Mention **two** things. (*7*) **2**

   ....

   ....

7 What else does he say about him? Mention **two** things. (*8*) **2**

   ....

   ....

8 What classes does he have on a Thursday morning? What does he think of them? (*9*) **4**

subject	opinion

9 What does he do on Wednesday lunchtimes? Mention **two** things. Why does he do this? (*10*) **3**

   He ....

   ....

   This is because ....

10 Why is he looking forward to this Friday? Mention **two** things. (*11*) **2**

    ....

    ....

2 Questions about family and daily routine

You will hear a series of questions related to family: before you listen, revise the vocabulary for daily routine and family members. You should also look at the vocabulary for household tasks, as well as words to describe people.

1 Who does Erich live with? Which ages does he mention? (*12*) **5**

person	age

2   Which members of his family does he mention? Mention **one** thing he
    says about each one.   (*13*)   **3**

family member	comment
1	
2	
3	

3   He describes his sister. Which of these people is his sister?   (*14*)   **1**

4   How does his morning routine work?   (*15*)   **3**

time	activity
6.15	
7.00	
7.30	

5   Who is he going to visit tomorrow?   (*16*)   **1**

    ....

6   What will they do there?   (*17*)   **1**

    ....

7   Why is next week special? Mention **two** things.   (*18*)   **2**

    ....
    ....

8 What does he have to do to help at home? Tick the correct activities.   (19)   **3**

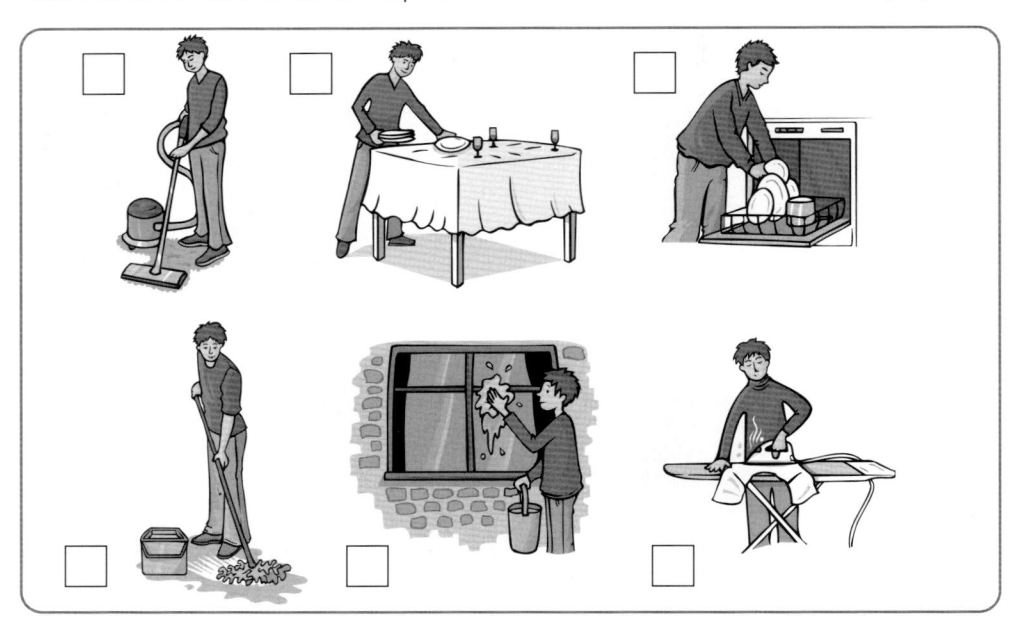

9 He mentions **two** things he does to earn extra pocket money.
   What are these activities? What does he think of them?   (20)   **4**

activities	opinion

10 You meet his sister: what **two** questions does she ask you?   (21)   **2**

	asked
How long are you here for?	
How long was your journey?	
How did you get to our house?	
What do you think of our house?	

3 Questions about home, food and drink

You will hear a series of questions related to houses, homes and rooms of the house: before you listen, revise the vocabulary for these topic areas. You should also look at the vocabulary for eating, drinking and shopping.

Chapter 7

1 Which of these houses does Brigitte live in? *(22)*   **1**

2 Which rooms does she mention in the house? Tick the box if she mentions the room. *(23)*   **4**

kitchen		living room	
bathroom		dining room	
bedroom		cellar	
utility room		attic	

3 What **three** things does she tell you about her house? *(24)*   **3**

Her house does not have ....

It does have a ....

Her house is very ....

LISTENING: FOUNDATION AND GENERAL LEVELS

41

4 Brigitte tells you about where her older sister, Lisa (a student), now lives: what information does she give you? Tick the correct boxes. *(25)* **3**

Her sister lives:

on the first floor	
on the ground floor	
in a flat with one bedroom	
alone	
with another student	
in a flat with a kitchen	
in a flat with a shower	

5 You are about to have lunch: what will you be having to eat? Choose the correct illustration. *(26)* **2**

6 Her mother asks you to go to the supermarket for her: what does she ask you to get? *(27)* **4**

a kilo of	
a tin of	
250 grammes of	
a bottle of	

Chapter 7

7   While you are at the supermarket, you decide to buy some chocolates to take home as a present: how much do they cost?   *(28)*   **1**

   ....

8   On the way home you meet Brigitte. She has a message to get, too: what must she buy? Where will she get this?   *(29)*   **2**

   She is going to buy .... at the ....

9   You are in the restaurant with your penfriend's parents: the waiter offers you a choice of accompaniments to your main course: what choices are you offered? Tick **three** boxes.   *(30)*   **3**

mixed salad	
tomato salad	
vegetables	
fried potatoes	
boiled potatoes	

10   Brigitte's father offers you a drink with your meal: what choices are you offered?   *(31)*   **3**

1	
2	
3	

4 Questions about work and hobbies

You will hear a series of questions related to free time and sport: before you listen, revise the vocabulary for these topic areas. You should also look at the vocabulary for jobs and professions.

1   Which of these hobbies does Saskia mention?   *(32)*   **3**

going to cinema		going out with friends	
cycling		horse riding	
swimming		reading	

2   What does she say about television?   *(33)*   **2**

   ....

LISTENING: FOUNDATION AND GENERAL LEVELS

3. On Wednesday afternoon Saskia is in two sport clubs: which ones does she mention? Tick **two** boxes. *(34)*   **2**

4. Saskia has two suggestions for you for tomorrow: what **two** things does she suggest you might like to do? *(35)*   **2**

   1 ....

   2 ....

5. This weekend you have the choice of two activities with Saskia's family: what are the **two** choices you are offered? *(36)*   **2**

   1 ....

   2 ....

6. You are invited out with Saskia's friends: where will you be going, how will you get there, and when will the event start? *(37)*   **3**

   You are going to ....

   You are going in ....

   It starts at ....

7. A friend of Saskia's tells you about his plans for the summer: where is he going? What is he going to do there? Mention **two** things. *(38)*   **3**

   He is going to ....

   There, he is going to ....

8 Saskia tells you about her part-time job: when does she work? How much does she earn? (*39*) **6**

days	and
times	until
earnings	per

9 Saskia's mother tells you about her job. Complete the sentences. (*40*) **3**

Her mother works as a .... She has done this for .... She works in ....

10 Saskia's mother tells you more about her job: what does she like and dislike about it? (*41*) **2**

Likes ....

Dislikes ....

5 Questions about transport and around town

You will hear a series of questions related to methods of transport and places in town: before you listen, revise the vocabulary for these topic areas. You should also look at the vocabulary for the weather.

1 Your penfriend, Dagmar, mentions how you are getting to school the next day. Which methods of transport will you use? Tick **three** boxes. (*42*) **3**

Chapter 7

2. Where exactly is her school? *(43)* — **2**

   Her school is in the ...., next to the ....

3. At what time does the bus leave to get you home?
   How much will it cost? *(44)* — **2**

   The bus leaves at .... Your ticket will cost ....

4. This Saturday your penfriend proposes an excursion: where to? How does she propose you get there? What will decide the method of transport you use? *(45)* — **5**

   You are going to ....

   You'll go by ....or ....

   You'll go by ....if ....

5. She tells you about the holiday she went on last year: how did she get there? What was the weather like? *(46)* — **3**

   She went by .... and ....

   The weather was ...., but ....

6. The school is organising a trip for you the next day: where are you going? How will you get there? What will you do? *(47)* — **3**

   The trip is to .... You are going there by ....

   There, you will ....

7. Your penfriend's mother suggests somewhere to go when you get back from school. Where does she suggest? How do you get there? *(48)* — **5**

   She suggests you go to .... It is ....
   away from here. Get off at ...., and it is in the ....
   street on the ....

8. You are looking for some German CDs to take home: where does Dagmar suggest you look? Mention **two** places. *(49)* — **2**

   ....

   ....

9. You are going to visit Dagmar's grandparents: where do they live?
   Fill in the blanks. *(50)* — **3**

   They live .... away. They live in a ....
   on ....

10 What does Dagmar think of where they live? Mention **one** advantage and
    one disadvantage. Why is the disadvantage a problem for them? *(51)*   3

    ....

    ....

Chapter 8

LISTENING: CREDIT LEVEL

At this level, the texts you hear will be longer, and there will be fewer guidelines on answering the questions. You should not assume that the person speaking will be a penfriend.

1 Talking about future plans

You will hear a series of questions related to a young person's plans for the future.

1   Stefan is about to leave school and go to university: why did he like school? Mention **three** things.   *(52)*   **3**

    ....
    ....
    ....

2   Where is he going to study? Mention **two** things about the place.   *(53)*   **3**

    ....
    ....
    ....

3   What does he say will be a problem when he's there? Give **four** details.   *(54)*   **4**

    ....
    ....
    ....

4   What plans does he have for this summer? Mention any **four** things.   *(55)*   **4**

    ....
    ....
    ....

5   What does he say about his life after university? Mention **three** details.   *(56)*   **3**

    ....
    ....
    ....

6   How will he support himself at university? Mention **three** things.   (57)   **3**

....
....
....

2 Talking about a visit

You will hear a series of questions related to a German girl's trip to another country.

1   Connie went to America; why did she go there? Mention **three** things.   (58)   **3**

....
....
....

2   Where exactly did she go? Mention **three** things about the place   (59)   **3**

....
....
....

3   Where did she stay while she was there? Give **four** details.   (60)   **4**

....
....
....

4   What problems did she have there? Mention any **three** things.   (61)   **3**

....
....
....

5   What does she say she liked most? Mention **three** details.   (62)   **3**

....
....
....

6   How is she in contact with America now she is back home? Mention **three** things.   (63)   **3**

....
....
....

Chapter 8

3 Interview with a young immigrant

You will hear a series of questions related to a young person who moved to Germany.

1. Boris moved to Germany when he was young. How did he feel about this? Mention **three** things. *(64)* — **3**

2. He used to live in Warsaw. Mention **three** things about his life there. *(65)* — **3**

3. Why did they come to Germany? Give **four** details. *(66)* — **4**

4. Why is he happier now? Mention any **three** things. *(67)* — **3**

5. What contact does he now have with Poland? Mention **three** details. *(68)* — **3**

6. Why will he stay here? What will he do? Mention **two** things. *(69)* — **3**

Chapter 9

TRANSCRIPTS AND ANSWERS TO THE LISTENING QUESTIONS

Transcripts: Foundation and General levels

1 Questions about school

1 Die Schule beginnt um Viertel vor acht, und ist um halb eins aus. Wir haben eine kleine Pause um zwanzig nach neun. Diese Pause ist zwanzig Minuten lang.

2 Wir haben von Montag bis Samstag Schule: Dienstag ist mein liebster Tag, denn ich habe nur drei Stunden. Ich hasse Samstag, weil am Wochenende schulfrei sein sollte.

3 Morgens stehe ich an Schultagen um Viertel nach sechs auf; und nach dem Frühstück fahre ich um sieben Uhr dreißig mit der Straßenbahn zur Schule.

4 Ich bin seit fünf Jahren auf dem Carl-Duisberg-Gymnasium und bin jetzt in der zehnten Klasse.

5 Mittwochs habe ich nachmittags Unterricht ab ein Uhr fünfunddreißig.

6 Mein Klassenlehrer heißt Herr Fitsch. Wir alle finden ihn sehr nett.

7 Er ist auch unser Sportlehrer. Er ist ziemlich alt, Mitte fünfzig, aber noch sehr fit!

8 Donnerstags habe ich Erdkunde, was ich ziemlich interessant finde. Danach habe ich eine Doppelstunde Französisch. Das finde ich aber total langweilig.

9 Weil ich nachmittags Unterricht habe, bleibe ich Mittwochs in der Stadt. Meinsteins gehe ich mit meinen Freunden Pommes essen.

10 Diese Woche ist Freitag aber ein toller Tag. Es ist der letzte Tag vor den Herbstferien.

2 Questions about family and daily routine

1 Ich wohne bei meiner Mutter, Irene, zusammen mit meiner Schwester Anja (sie ist zwölf Jahre alt) und meinem grossen Bruder Hugo. Er ist einundzwanzig und geht auf die Uni.

2 Mein Vater wohnt in Berlin. Meine kleine Schwester ist immer sehr guter Laune. Von meinem Bruder sehe ich aber leider nicht sehr viel, er ist nie zu Hause.

3 Meine Schwester Anja ist sehr schlank, sie hat lange lockige dunkelbraune Haare.

4 Morgens stehe ich um Viertel nach sechs auf. Um sieben Uhr stehe ich unter der Dusche. Um halb acht verlasse ich das Haus.

5 Morgen wollen wir meine Oma besuchen.

6 Einmal pro Woche treffen wir uns zu Kaffee und Kuchen bei ihr.

7 Nächste Woche ist aber ein besonderer Tag. Oma hat Geburtstag. Sie wird vierundsechzig Jahre alt.

8 Ich mache ziemlich viel zu Hause. Jeden Tag tue ich das Geschirr in die Spülmaschine, und decke den Tisch. Alle zwei Tage muss ich staubsaugen.

9 Ich arbeite auch, um mehr Taschengeld zu kriegen. Jede Woche putze ich die Fenster, was ich nicht sehr gern mache. Ich führe auch den Hund spazieren, das mache ich lieber, denn ich gehe zusammen mit Olli und seinem Hund.

10 Hallo! Wie lange war die Reise von Schottland? Wie findest du unser Haus?

3 Questions about home, food and drink

1 Ich wohne in einem Reihenhaus am Stadtrand.

2 Wir haben ein Wohnzimmer, drei Schlafzimmer, einen Keller und auch eine Waschküche.

3 Wir haben keine Garage, aber hinter dem Haus gibt es einen großen Garten. Unser Haus ist sehr ruhig gelegen.

4 Meine Schwester Lisa wohnt jetzt in München; sie ist Studentin. Sie hat eine kleine Wohnung, die sie mit einer anderen Studentin teilt. Die Wohnung ist im ersten Stock und hat eine Dusche aber keine Küche: sie muss im Wohnzimmer kochen.

5 Heute gibt es Hähnchen mit Salat. Als Nachspeise haben wir Obst.

6 Könntest du für mich einkaufen gehen? Wir brauchen ein Kilo Kartoffeln, eine Dose Tomaten, 250 Gramm Holländerkäse und eine Flasche Apfelsaft.

7 Die Pralinen kosten elf Euro fünfzig.

8 Hallo. Ich muss zur Apotheke. Kommst du mit? Ich will Kopfschmerztabletten kaufen.

9 Als Beilage haben wir einen gemischtens Salat, gegrilltes Gemüse oder Salzkartoffeln.

10 Was trinkst du lieber? Möchtest du Orangensaft, Cola oder ein Glas Rotwein?

4 Questions about work and hobbies

1 In meiner Freizeit treffe ich mich gern mit meinen Freunden. Ich lese auch viel und ich fahre Rad.

2 Ich sehe nicht oft fern, weil ich zu viele Hausaufgaben habe.

3 Ich bin Mitglied in einem Volleyballverein und zweimal pro Woche gehe ich zum Fitnessraum.

4 Morgen möchte ich in Frankfurt einkaufen gehen: am Abend könnten wir dann ins Kino gehen.

5 Am Wochenende wollten wir in die Berge gehen, um eine Wanderung zu machen. Oder möchtest du lieber eine Bootsfahrt auf dem Rhein machen?

6 Heute Abend geht eine Gruppe aus der Klasse auf ein Rockkonzert: Uschis Vater bringt uns mit seinem Wagen dahin. Es beginnt um zwanzig Uhr.

7 Diesen Sommer fahre ich mit zwei Freunden in die Schweiz. Da werden wir einen Segelkurs machen. Wir wohnen eine Woche lang in einem Zelt.

8 Ich habe einen Nebenjob: ich arbeite Dienstag – und Donnerstag nachmittag, von vierzehn bis siebzehn Uhr dreißig. Ich passe auf die Kinder meiner Nachbarin auf und bekomme fünf Euro die Stunde.

9 Ich arbeite als Krankenschwester: ich arbeite seit acht Jahren in einem Altersheim hier in der Stadt.

10 Ich mag meine Arbeit gern, denn ich arbeite immer von acht bis drei Uhr und muss nie Nachts arbeiten. Es kann aber manchmal ein wenig stressig sein.

5 Questions about transport and around town

1 Morgen bringt Mutti uns im Auto zur Bushaltestelle, wir fahren zehn Minuten mit dem Bus zum Marktplatz und laufen dann fünf Minuten zu Fuß zur Schule.

2 Die Schule ist in der Stadtmitte neben dem Rathaus.

3 Morgen ist Mittwoch: wir fahren um zehn vor eins mit dem Bus nach Hause. Die Fahrt kostet für dich ein Euro zwanzig.

4 Samstag könnten wir ins Freibad gehen. Wir könnten entweder das Fahrrad nehmen oder zu Fuß gehen. Wenn es richtig heiß ist, dann fahren wir lieber mit dem Rad.

5 Letzten Sommer sind wir nach Helgoland gefahren: wir sind mit der Bahn und dann mit der Fähre gefahren. Das Wetter war schön: es hat nie geregnet, es war aber an zwei Tagen sehr windig.

6 Morgen hat die Schule für uns einen Tagesausflug organisiert: wir fahren mit der Bahn zum Hamburger Hafen. Da machen wir eine Hafenrundfahrt in einem Boot.

7 Wenn du Lust hast, kannst du heute Nachmittag ins Hallenbad gehen. Es ist eine halbe Stunde von hier mit der Straßenbahn. Du steigst am Park aus, und das Hallenbad ist in der ersten Straße links.

8 Also für CDs: entweder gehst du zum Kaufhaus in der Stadtmitte, oder du kannst zum Musikladen am Marktplatz gehen.

9 Oma und Opa wohnen etwa dreißig Kilometer entfernt. Sie haben eine Wohnung am Stadtrand von Pinneberg.

10 Da, wo sie wohnen, ist es sehr schön und ruhig: es gibt aber keine Geschäfte in der Nähe. Das ist ein Problem, da sie kein Auto haben.

Chapter 9

Transcripts: Credit level

1 Talking about future plans

1. Ich war neun Jahre auf dieser Schule: ich habe die Schule sehr gern gernocht, denn ich hatte hier viele gute Freunde. Ich kam mit den Lehrern meistens sehr gut aus und schließlich bekam ich eine gute Note in meinem Abitur.

2. Ich gehe jetzt auf die Uni in München: München selbst ist eine riesengroße Stadt, und ich weiß, da ist sehr viel los für junge Leute.

3. Das Problem an München ist, dass alles da sehr teuer für mich sein wird. Ein Zimmer wird mich sehr viel kosten, die Preise in den Kneipen sind auch viel höher als hier zu Hause, und man muss mit hohen Transportkosten rechnen, da die Stadt so groß ist.

4. Diesen Sommer muss ich also arbeiten, damit ich ein wenig Geld für meine Zeit in Bayern habe. Mein Onkel hat für mich eine Stelle gefunden: ich arbeite in einer Fabrik, wo er durch seine Arbeit gute Kontakte hat.

5. Nach der Uni hoffe ich in der Welt herumreisen zu können. Ich möchte zuerst in den Vereinigten Staaten jobben, vielleicht in Kalifornien. Ich will natürlich mein eigenes Geld verdienen und nicht immer von meinen Eltern abhängig sein.

6. Ich weiß, ich werde auch während der Uni jobben müssen. Ich werde vielleicht eine Stelle als Taxifahrer am Wochenende suchen. Ich habe gehört, man kann hundert Euro pro Nacht verdienen. In den Semesterferien werde ich natürlich nach Hause kommen, um in der Fabrik zu arbeiten.

2 Talking about a visit

1. Ich war vor zwei Jahren mit der Schule in den USA. Unsere Schule hatte einen Austausch mit einem amerikanischen College. Meine Eltern dachten, es wäre gut für mich, mal in Amerika auf eine Schule zu gehen, und die Reise war nicht besonders teuer.

2. Wir waren in einer kleinen Stadt an der Ostküste der USA. Die Stadt, Hamilton, hat 20 000 Einwohner und liegt etwa hundert Kilometer von Boston entfernt.

3. Ich war bei einer amerikanischen Familie. Der Vater war Zahnarzt, also war die Familie ziemlich wohlhabend. Ihr Haus hatte zwei Stockwerke und fünfzehn Zimmer! Sie hatten ihren eigenes Pool, was sehr entspannend war.

4. Ich habe bemerkt, dass man in den USA sehr große Mengen isst. Ich konnte nie alles, was auf meinem Teller war, aufessen. Ich bin daran gewöhnt, viel Obst und Gemüse zu essen. Da musste ich bei jeder Mahlzeit Fleisch essen, was ich eigentlich nicht mochte.

5. Was mir am meisten gefallen hat, war die Freiheit. Schüler dürfen schon ab sechzehn Auto fahren, und sie machen auch viele Picknicks am Strand, obwohl der Strand zehn Kilometer weit weg ist! Abends gingen wir oft ins Kino und kamen erst um elf Uhr nach Hause.

6 Ich schreibe meiner Austauschpartnerin noch immer E-Mails, und wir sprechen oft am Telefon, aber nicht mit unseren Handys, weil das viel zu teuer ist! Die Emily kommt nächsten Sommer mit ihrer Schule, um uns zu besuchen. Ich freue mich richtig darauf!

3 Interview with a young immigrant

1 Ich bin mit meiner Familie vor sieben Jahren nach Deutschland gekommen. Früher wohnten wir in Polen. Am Anfang war es sehr schwer, weil ich überhaupt kein Deutsch konnte, außerdem vermisste ich all meine Freunde.

2 Wir wohnten in Warschau, der polnischen Hauptstadt. Wir hatten ein eigenes Haus mit Garten, und alle meine Freunde wohnten in der Umgebung. Meine Kusinen wohnten auch um die Ecke.

3 Wir sind in eine kleine Wohnung hier in Köln gezogen. Mein Vater wollte hier eine bessere Arbeit finden. Er ist Elektriker, und er dachte, er könnte hier mehr Geld verdienen und ein besseres Leben aufbauen als zu Hause.

4 Jetzt geht es uns viel besser. Wir haben eine größere Wohnung, und ich habe viele neue Freunde gefunden. Ich bekomme gute Noten in der Schule und hoffe später studieren zu können.

5 Wir fahren jeden Sommer nach Warschau zurück, um meine Großeltern zu besuchen. Meine Kusinen wohnen jetzt auch in Deutschland, nicht sehr weit weg von uns. Meine Eltern werden in fünf Jahren nach Polen zurückfahren, und im alten Haus wohnen.

6 Ich glaube aber, ich werde hier bleiben. Ich habe eine Freundin, die ich vermissen würde! Ich will hier studieren, und dann vielleicht in Berlin eine Arbeit suchen. Berlin ist nicht zu weit weg von Warschau.

Answers: Foundation and General levels

1 Questions about school

1

start	7.45
finish	12.30
break starts	9.20
length of break	20 minutes

Chapter 9

2

	school?	favourite	not so good!
Monday	✓		
Tuesday	✓	✓	
Wednesday	✓		
Thursday	✓		
Friday	✓		
Saturday	✓		✓

3 He gets up at **6.15** and goes to school by **tram**.

4 He has been there for **five years**. He is in the **tenth** class.

5 Classes start at **1.35**.

6 Herr Fitsch **is his form/class teacher; they all like him/he is very nice**.

7 He is also **their PE teacher**, he is **quite old (mid-fifties)** but **still fit** (any two).

8

subject	opinion
geography	interesting
double French	boring

9 He stays in town and **eats chips/eats with his friends**. This is because he **has classes in the afternoon**.

10 It is the **last day before the autumn holidays**.

2 Questions about family and daily routine

1

person	age
mother	
sister	12
brother	21

2

	family member	comment
1	father	lives in Berlin
2	sister	always in a good mood
3	brother	doesn't see much of him/never at home

3

4

time	activity
6.15	gets up
7.00	showers
7.30	leaves house

5 **his grandmother**

6 **have coffee and cakes**

7 It is his **grandmother's birthday, she will be 64**.

8

9

activities	opinion
cleans windows	doesn't like this
walks the dog	likes/prefers this

10

	asked
How long are you here for?	
How long was your journey?	✓
How did you get to our house?	
What do you think of our house?	✓

3 Questions about home, food and drink

1

2

kitchen		living room	✓
bathroom		dining room	
bedroom	✓	cellar	✓
utility room	✓	attic	

3 Her house does not have **a garage**. It does have a **garden**. Her house is very **quiet**.

4

on the first floor	✓
on the ground floor	
in a flat with one bedroom	
alone	
with another student	✓
in a flat with a kitchen	
in a flat with a shower	✓

5

6

a kilo of	**potatoes**
a tin of	**tomatoes**
250 grammes of	**cheese**
a bottle of	**apple juice**

7 **€11.50**

8 She is going to buy **headache pills** at the **chemist's**.

9

mixed salad	✓
tomato salad	
vegetables	✓
fried potatoes	
boiled potatoes	✓

10

1	orange juice
2	Coke
3	a glass of (red) wine

4 Questions about work and hobbies

1

going to cinema		going out with friends	✓
cycling	✓	horse riding	
swimming		reading	✓

2 **She doesn't watch much television because she has too much homework.**

3

4 **She suggests going shopping (in Frankfurt) and going to the cinema.**

5 **She suggests walking/going to the mountains or a boat trip (on the Rhine).**

6 You are going to **a (rock) concert**. You are going in **Uschi's (father's) car**. It starts at **8p.m**.

7 He is going to **Switzerland**. There, he is going to **learn to sail** and **stay in a tent**.

8

days	**Tuesday** and **Thursday**
times	**2p.m.** until **5.30p.m.**
earnings	**€5** per **hour**

9 Her mother works as a **nurse**. She has done this for **eight years**. She works in **an old people's home** (or **here in town**).

10 Likes: **works from 8a.m. until 3p.m., never has to work nights** (any one)

Dislikes: **can be stressful**

5 Questions about transport and around town

1

2 Her school is in the **town centre** next to the **town hall**.

3 The bus leaves at **12.50**. Your ticket will cost **€1.20**.

4 You are going to **the (open air) swimming pool**.

You'll go by **bike** or **on foot**.

You'll go by **bike** if **it's hot**.

5 She went by **train** and **ferry**.

The weather was **good (it didn't rain)** but **it was windy (on two days)**.

Chapter 9

6 The trip is to **the harbour/Hamburg**.
   You are going there by **train**.
   There, you will have a **boat trip around the harbour**.
7 She suggests you go to **the swimming pool**.
   It is **half an hour** away from here.
   Get off at **the park**, and it is in the **first** street on the **left**.
8 **The department store in the centre of town, the music shop in the market place**.
9 They live **30 kilometres** away.
   They live in a **flat** on **the edge of town/Pinneberg**.
10 **It is very nice/quiet, but there are no shops nearby. They don't have a car.**

Answers: Credit level

1 Talking about future plans

1 he had lots of friends
   he got on well with the teachers
   he got good marks in his (final) exams
2 he is going to Munich
   it is a very big city, there is lots for young people (any two)
3 it is very expensive
   a room will cost a lot
   prices in the pubs are higher than at home
   transport is expensive
4 he wants to work
   he wants to earn money for going to university (in Bavaria)
   his uncle found him a job
   he will work in a factory
   his uncle has contacts in the factory (any four)
5 he wants to travel
   he would like to work in the USA (California)
   he wants to earn money/be independent from his parents
6 he'll look for a weekend job as a taxi driver
   he can earn €100 a night
   in the vacations he'll come home to work

Chapter 9

2 Talking about a visit

1. her school had an exchange
   her parents thought it was a good idea to go to an American school
   the trip was not too expensive
2. a small town on the east coast
   it (Hamilton) had 20,000 inhabitants
   it was 100 kilometres from Boston
3. with an American family
   the father was a dentist
   the family was well off
   the house had two floors/fifteen rooms
   it had its own swimming pool (any four)
4. people ate a lot
   she could never finish the food on her plate
   she was used to eating fruit/vegetables
   she didn't like eating meat at every meal (any three)
5. she liked the freedom
   people could drive at age sixteen
   they went for picnics on the beach (which was 10 kilometres away)
   they went to the cinema and came home late (11p.m.) (any three)
6. she writes e-mails
   they phone often
   they don't use their mobile phones because it's too expensive

3 Interview with a young immigrant

1. he found it hard
   he knew no German
   he missed his friends
2. they had their own house and garden
   his friends lived nearby
   his cousins lived around the corner
3. his father was looking for a better job
   he was an electrician
   he thought he could earn more money
   he thought they could have a better life

63

4 they have a bigger flat
   he has lots of new friends
   he gets good marks at school
5 they go back every summer to visit his grandparents
   his cousins now live in Germany, not far away
   his parents will return to Poland in five years' time
6 he has a girlfriend he would miss
   he wants to study here
   he will look for a job in Berlin

Chapter 10

SPEAKING

Speaking is worth **one-third** of your overall Standard Grade result because it is such a key skill. You will have to carry out three speaking assessments over the course of the year before your exams: these assessments will be set by your teacher, and will also be marked by your teacher. They may be recorded, or they may not. This is a part of the course you can really prepare for, and do very well in, if you get the preparation right!

Your teacher will take the marks for your three tests and make an average of them: this will be your final speaking grade. If you have one poorer assessment, it isn't the end of the world; the others can bring up your average.

The rules for the assessments are quite clear: there will be three different types of assessment. One will be a **prepared talk** or presentation, on a subject of your choice. You will have to speak with a certain number of words allowed as notes to help you through. Your talk will be graded according to content, accuracy and a few other elements. The way of judging how well you have done is given in the grade-related criteria your teacher will be working from: these are shown on page 72, so that you can see what is expected of you.

The second assessment will be an informal **conversation**: this will normally involve using either *du* or *Sie*, and talking about a subject you will know in advance and can prepare. It could be the same subject you have covered for your prepared talk. There are different grade-related criteria for this, which we have included for you on page 77.

The third assessment will be a **role play**, a transactional or vocational task in which you take part in a dialogue with an adult speaker of German (this may of course be your teacher!), but for this task you will have to use *Sie*. This will be polite, formal or vocational language. The grade-related criteria for this are the same as those for the conversation (see page 77).

You will know the topics for the more formal assessments beforehand so you can prepare for them. This is a huge advantage!

In this chapter we will look at the three types of task in detail, and give you advice and support on preparing for the kind of task you are likely to be given.

Chapter 10

The prepared talk

For this assessment, you will have to talk on a subject of your choice for up to two minutes: you can prepare this well in advance, and learn it so that you can be absolutely sure of what you have to do. You are also allowed to have some notes to speak from, and it is worthwhile thinking about how you will use this opportunity.

To get a General award, you will have to speak for at least a minute: you will also have to try to use a variety of tenses and structures. You should be able to give your opinion on various parts of your experience. Try to be as accurate as you can.

For Credit, you will have to speak for up to two minutes. You must be reasonably accurate in your use of German, and use tenses and word order well. Your opinions will be more important than at General level, and should also include reasons for some of these opinions.

Planning your talk

When you have a subject for your assessment, try to break it down into three or more sections, and prepare each one separately: this will make it easier to remember. You are allowed five headings, of eight words each, as support, so these key words should settle you into each section of your talk. This is handy because if you get nervous and a bit mixed up in one part, you can recover in the next part with the help of your key words.

Once you've chosen your topic area, focus on the actual language you will use. Here are a few do's and don'ts!

Do's

- Do look at the textbook or texts you are working from for good ideas you can use.
- Do make sure you understand what you are saying, or it will be very difficult to remember it properly.
- Do show a draft to your teacher, to get any suggestions, or so that you can make corrections.
- Do use a variety of structures: don't start off every sentence with *Ich*, for example.
- Do vary your tenses, and put in some joining words like *weil* or *wenn*.
- Do give your opinion, and work at using different ways to say what you think. Look at the section on giving opinions in Chapter 12.

Chapter 10

Don'ts ✓

- Don't leave the preparation to the last minute! If you start your preparation early, you'll be able to ask your teacher for advice on any vocabulary or grammar you're unsure of.
- Don't always stick to safe, simple language. It may be easier, but it won't get the best grades. Try out some of the more impressive sentences you've learned. Note down useful vocabulary and phrases you've seen elsewhere under appropriate topic headings, so that you can reuse them in your speaking tests.
- Don't use lists of things, such as school subjects, places in town or favourite foods to try to make your talk longer: this will count against you.

To help you prepare for a solo talk, we have selected three possible topics and will guide you through the process involved in preparing for and carrying out the assessment. You can follow the same pattern for a topic of your own choice. You might also find Chapter 11 on writing useful to help you prepare for a specific speaking task.

1 An exchange visit
2 Fernsehen
3 Meine Schule

1 An exchange visit

You have been asked to present a solo talk about an exchange visit. Sort out your ideas and choose the areas you feel most confident about, for example, your exchange partner's house or family, the school you visited or how you got there. You'll then find it easier to prepare each area in more detail. For a General award, you can either concentrate on two of these areas, or give shorter answers to each of the three.

Look at the vocabulary and language you have in your textbooks and material you have from school, and take what you think might help you. Look also at the suggested structures in Chapter 12, and take a few you think will fit in with what you are going to say.

Once you have chosen the kinds of things you are going to say, let us take the first section. You might decide to talk about how you got to your partner's house. This will allow you to use the past tense, to describe your journey. You can fit in time and place words and phrases. You will also be able to use the vocabulary for methods of transport you know, and give your opinions on these. You can introduce a couple of good structures, too, to show you know lots of good German! Here is an example of the kind of thing you can say:

Letztes Jahr bin ich nach Dortmund in Deutschland gefahren, wo mein Briefpartner wohnt. Ich bin mit einer Schulgruppe gefahren: wir waren 28 mit drei Lehrern. Die Reise war sehr lang, denn wir sind mit dem Bus gefahren. Wir sind nicht durch den Eurotunnel gefahren, sondern mit der Fähre. Die Reise war aber okay, denn all meine Freunde waren da, und ich hatte meinen Xbox und Walkman.

This would take about half a minute to say, and you would be working at Credit level. You could shorten and simplify it, so that it would take fifteen to twenty seconds, and you would still be working at General level. Once you have produced the first part, choose the key words that you will use to help you when you carry out your presentation. This could be the first few words of your talk, to get you started, or key words from throughout the different sections, or a phrase which you always find hard to remember exactly. What is important is that it helps you remember your talk better.

The second section could be about the school your penfriend goes to. This paragraph can be in the present tense, and allows you to compare a German school to your own school, and to give opinions. Look at the vocabulary given, and try to put together your own paragraph. Make sure you put in some opinions and comparisons!

Es gibt keine Bibliothek oder Kantine.	*There is no library or dinner hall.*
Sie haben das Recht, die Schule zu verlassen.	*They are allowed to go out of school.*
Wir haben das Recht, in der Schule zu essen.	*We are allowed to eat in school.*
Sie müssen ihre Hefte selbst kaufen.	*They have to buy their own jotters.*
Es gibt … Schüler und … Lehrer.	*There are … pupils and … teachers.*
Man braucht keine Schuluniform zu tragen.	*You don't have to wear school uniform.*
Schule beginnt um … und endet um …	*School starts at … and finishes at …*
Es ist ein großes, modernes Gebäude.	*It is a large modern building.*
Es ist eine Gesamtschule.	*It is a comprehensive school.*

When you are doing this, remember not to produce a list of things the school has, and try to vary the language. Here is an example of what you could say:

Die Schule meines Briefpartners ist ein großes, altes Gebäude in der Stadtmitte. Die Schüler haben ihr eigenes Klassenzimmer! Es gibt 1 600 Schüler auf der Schule. Die Schule beginnt um Viertel vor acht, was viel zu früh ist, finde ich. Sie haben überhaupt keine Schuluniform, und tragen meistens Jeans und Sportschuhe auf der Schule: das sieht komisch aus.

Finally, you could prepare a section on your penfriend's home town and family. Here are some words and phrases you could work from:

Sie sind fünf in der Familie.	There are five people in his/her family.
Er hat … Brüder und … Schwestern.	He has … brothers and … sisters.
Er hat keine Geschwister.	He doesn't have any brothers and sisters.
seine/ihre Eltern, sein/ihr Vater, seine/ihre Mutter.	his/her parents, his/her father, his/her mother
Seine/Ihre Eltern sind sehr nett.	His/Her parents are very nice.
Ich komme mit seiner Mutter gut aus.	I get on well with his mother.
Seine/Ihre Stadt liegt im Norden.	His/Her town is in the north.
Sie ist mittelgroß.	It's a medium-sized town.
25 Kilometer von Dortmund	25 kilometres (15 miles) from Dortmund
Es gibt viel zu tun, wo er wohnt.	There are lots of things to do in his town.

This last section is also very much in the present tense, but in the sample answer below we have finished off with a different tense, the conditional. It also allows us to use the third person, varying our structures.

Mein Briefpartner wohnt nicht weit von der Stadtmitte in der Stadt, wo er wohnt. Er hat keine Geschwister, seine Eltern sind aber ganz nett. Ich habe mich mit allen sehr gut verstanden. Die Stadt ist im Nordwesten, etwa 30 Kilometer von Dortmund entfernt. Sie ist eine Industriestadt, aber sehr sauber und nett. Es gibt viel mehr zu tun als bei uns! Ich möchte nächstes Jahr wieder dahin fahren.

And remember: this solo talk could also double as one of your writing assessments!

2 Fernsehen

This topic will allow you to talk in both the first and the third person, use lots of opinion words, and use good phrases from the texts you are working from, so your first task should be to look at your source texts and select some phrases. Then, break your task into areas. In one section, you could talk about what you and other young people in Scotland actually watch on TV. You could also have a section in which you talk about how watching too much TV can be a danger to your health and social life. You could finish off by saying what you think TV should be like. If you have some material on what people watch in Germany, you could use this as well as or instead of the ideas above. Again, for a General award, you might find you have enough material in the first two sections. Remember to look at Chapter 12 to see how to give your opinion.

The first section allows you to use some longer sentences, and joining words like *wenn* and *um ... zu*. It might sound something like this:

> *Ich sehe jeden Tag fern. Wenn ich von der Schule nach Hause komme, sehe ich dann gern eine Seifenoper wie „Nachbarn". Ich sehe auch gern Sportsendungen, und meine Freunde kommen oft zu meinem Haus, um ein Fußballspiel zu sehen. Ich kann den ganzen Abend vor dem Fernseher sitzen, wenn ich keine Hausaufgaben habe.*

The next section is where you could put in your opinions, while explaining the dangers of watching too much TV. This would help you to a Credit award.

> *Es ist aber gefährlich, zu oft und zu viel fernzusehen. Man kann ganz schnell unfit werden, und, wenn du vor dem Fernseher bist, willst du immer etwas essen. Man sieht auch viele dumme Sendungen, und man kann vergessen zu denken. Die meisten Sendungen sind auch nicht sehr gut, und es wäre oft besser auszugehen, um mit seinen Freunden zu treffen.*

For a General award, it might be easier to go for simpler statements about what you like and don't like: if you added this next section to the previous one above, that would be enough. You could say something like this:

> *Meine Lieblingssendungen sind Musiksendungen, besonders die Sendungen auf Sky: ich sehe auch gern Filme und Krimis. Ich sehe nicht gern die Nachrichten, und ich finde Dokumentarfilme langweilig. Ich hasse politische Sendungen, weil ich Politik total uninteressant finde.*

In the third section, you have the chance to use different ways of expressing opinions, to put in a different tense or two, and to suggest how TV could be improved.

> *Als ich jünger war, dachte ich, dass das Fernsehen ziemlich gut war. Jetzt denke ich nicht mehr so. Wir sollen bessere Sendungen haben, besonders Musiksendungen für junge Leute. Mein Freund hat Satellitenfernsehen, und er kann viel mehr gute Sendungen als ich sehen. Ich möchte auch viel mehr gute Fußballspiele sehen, und nicht immer zu meinem Freund gehen, weil er Satellit hat.*

3 Meine Schule

This is a tricky topic to choose, as it is very easy to produce too simple a piece of German on the subject. It can also be tempting to go for lists of subjects and teachers, which is a bad idea. So it is very important that you choose areas which will allow you to use a variety of structures, and also to use your vocabulary. When deciding what to talk about, you might go for what you like and what you don't like at school: this allows you to express opinions and give explanations. The final section, for those working towards a Credit award, could be a wish list of things you would like to see happen to you or your school in the future. This also allows you to use different tenses, including the future and the conditional. Here is the kind of thing you might say if talking about what you don't like about school:

> *Was ich nicht bei meiner Schule mag? Ich glaube, dass ich viel zu viele Hausaufgaben habe: ich sitze jeden Abend zwei Stunden lang an dem Schreibtisch. Ich mag auch nicht die Kantine: das Essen ist fürchterlich, und die Kantine ist auch zu voll und zu laut. Wenn ich kann, gehe ich mit meinen Freunden in die Stadt. Ich esse dann ein Butterbrot oder Pommes Frites, obwohl ich weiß, das ist nicht sehr gesund. Wenn ich in der Kantine esse, dann nehme ich normalerweise einen Salat.*

This gives you the chance to use some longer sentences and joining words, and to show that you know where the verbs go. It also has some opinions. For a General award, it could be slightly simplified, to make it easier to remember.

You could then go on to say what you like about your school. Remember that you do not have to tell the whole truth when producing a speaking assessment: just avoid saying ridiculous things, as that might count against you. There are lots of chances here to give reasons to back up your opinions, and to use joining words, and you can finish with something to make the examiner happy:

> *Im Großen und Ganzen gehe ich gern in die Schule, denn all meine Freunde sind da. Meine Klassen sind meistens okay und ich finde die Lehrer nicht schlecht. Mein Lieblingsfach ist Musik, weil ich auch privat die Gitarre spiele, und ich kann in der Schule mit meinen Klassenkameraden üben. Ich finde Deutsch auch ziemlich gut, weil ich hier gute Noten habe.*

Finally, a chance to show you can use future and conditional tenses: you don't have to use a lot of these, just one or two to show that you know how they work. The first two sentences give opinions and reasons, and have verbs all over the place: make sure you understand why they are where they are, or you will find it difficult to produce this yourself. If you aren't sure, look at the sections on tenses and word order in Chapter 12.

> *Nächstes Jahr werde ich auf der Schule bleiben, weil ich meine Highers machen möchte. Ich möchte später auf die Uni gehen, wo ich Sportmedizin studieren will. Wir haben nicht genug Freiheit, und die Lehrer handeln uns oft wie kleine Kinder: hoffentlich ist das nächstes Jahr anders, und wir können mehr Freiheit haben.*

Chapter 10

Grade-related criteria for speaking: prepared talk

Although short talks (of up to one minute) may be the norm in performances at Foundation level, longer talks should be the norm at General and Credit levels (up to a maximum of two minutes).

Foundation	General	Credit
◆ Talks are limited and may be unfocused or lacking in structure.	◆ Talks go beyond basic content and show evidence of structure and/or focus.	◆ Talks are comprehensive in content, well structured and/or focused.
Candidates:	***Candidates:***	***Candidates:***
◆ can make a short presentation on a prepared topic ◆ can make themselves understood, although there may be mispronunciation, incorrect intonation, other-tongue interference, hesitation and quite frequent grammatical error ◆ have a limited range of vocabulary, structures and phrases ◆ tend to repeat structures and/or whole phrases ◆ may express simple opinions	◆ can speak at some length on a prepared topic ◆ can communicate with some success and accuracy in basic structures, although there may be some mispronunciation and weakness in intonation, grammatical errors and occasional hesitation ◆ may attempt a range of tenses and/or vocabulary ◆ can express opinions and reasons as required ◆ may make an attempt at a wider range of vocabulary, phrases and structures with frequent error or may speak carefully and deliberately but be more accurate	◆ can make a full and comprehensive presentation on a prepared topic ◆ have no difficulty making themselves understood ◆ can use the language flexibly and are generally accurate although there may be occasional grammatical errors particularly in more complex language ◆ express opinions and reasons well and may expand on them ◆ have generally correct intonation and pronunciation

Grade 6	Grade 5	Grade 4	Grade 3	Grade 2	Grade 1
Talks tend to be short, limited in range, unfocused and very inaccurate.	Talks may be short and limited in range, but are more focused and accurate.	Talks may be inaccurate with reasonable range, or more accurate but lacking in range.	Talks are more accurate and vocabulary and structures are more wide ranging.	Talks are mostly accurate but ideas are less well developed, or ideas are better developed but talks are less accurate.	Candidates are able to speak at some length, showing both development of ideas and control of the language.

Chapter 10

The conversation

Preparing for the conversation is not really very different from preparing for the solo talk: you will know what topic area you are going to discuss, and you will be able to make sure you have answers ready for any questions you are asked on this topic. You will not need to remember a big piece of text, but you will have to recognise which question needs which answer! You can also ask your own questions, and you should be ready to deal with the unexpected: this is not as difficult as it sounds, as there is a set of things you can do to help yourself.

First, you need to know the question words, so that you know what is being asked of you. Here are the main ones you will meet:

Wer? (*also*: Mit wem?)	*Who? (also: Who with?)*
Was?	*What?*
Wann?	*When?*
Wo?	*Where?*
Welcher/Welche/Welches?	*Which?*
Warum?	*Why?*
Wann?	*How?*
Wie viel/Wie viele?	*How much/How many?*
Wie lange?	*How long?*
Um wie viel Uhr?	*At what time?*

Remember that, in English, we use 'Do' to make a question: Do you have, Do you know, and so on. In German, this is not necessary: normally the question will be asked using **inversion**, that is, changing the order of the subject and the object: *Hast du? Bist du?* This means that questions should look like this:

Wann beginnt die Schule?	*When does school start?*
Wo wohnst du?	*Where do you live?*

This rule doesn't apply when an English question has an auxiliary in it: have, are, can, should, etc. Here, German questions work exactly the same as English ones:

SPEAKING

Chapter 10

> Warum bist du zu Hause?
> Wann kannst du gehen?
>
> *Why are you at home?*
> *When can you go?*

What else do we have to think about? As for the prepared talk, your teacher will assess you using the grade-related criteria, which are given on page 77. You should look at the level you are aiming for, and then make sure you show that you can do the things you need to do. Think about what the criteria mean. Here are some of them from the Credit list.

Candidates:	What you need to do:
◆ readily take initiative	This means you should ask questions too, or change the subject: use the guide to questions above to help you.
◆ express agreement, disagreement, opinions and reasons well and can expand on them if required	Remember to give opinions, and reasons for them: look at the solo talk section for more help on this.
◆ have no difficulty making themselves understood and can use the language flexibly, coping well with unexpected questions	Be ready to say – *Ich habe nicht verstanden* and *Wie bitte?* to give you time to think.
◆ are generally accurate although there may be occasional grammatical errors and weaknesses in pronunciation	Make sure your preparation gives you lots of good material, which you have checked and learned in advance.
◆ speak with little hesitation, other-tongue interference or weakness in intonation	Being prepared is all-important!
◆ can use a range of language structures with some confidence	Make sure you have good structures prepared for your answers: think about word order.
◆ may attempt a range of tenses	Think about tenses when preparing your answers! And remember where your verbs go.

Let us look at the topic *Fernsehen*, which was used on page 70 to demonstrate a solo talk. On page 75, there is a list of possible questions you might be asked in a conversation on the same topic. They use different ways of asking questions, but that won't affect your answers. Try to put your own answers to the questions, using the vocabulary you know from studying this area, and remembering to refer to the guidelines on giving your opinion in Chapter 12. Then have a look at the sample answers on page 76. Remember that this is a conversation, so you should be ready to ask some of these questions yourself. You can either just ask them, or, if you have just been asked one, say *Und du?* after your answer, then repeat the question. Don't do this all the time, or you are unlikely to get a Credit grade.

If your teacher is playing the part of a young person, or your test is with another student, use *du*. If, however, your test is with an adult, remember to change *Und du?* to *Und Sie?* and change also the form of the verb. You will find more help on asking questions with *Sie* in the role-play section.

Ist Fernsehen dir wichtig?

Warum?

Wie findest du Fernsehen?

Sieht deine Familie oft fern?

Wie findest du Seifenopern?

Was siehst du gern?

Was magst du nicht?

Was ist deine Lieblingssendung?

Wie oft siehst du fern?

Hast du gestern Abend ferngesehen?

Chapter 10

Questions	Sample answers
Ist Fernsehen dir wichtig?	Ja, es ist mir sehr wichtig.
Warum? (This is what you will be asked if you answered Ja to the previous question.)	Weil ich über die Sendungen mit meinen Freunden spreche. (This is a chance to show structures.)
Wie findest du Fernsehen? (Whatever your answer, try to say at least two things.)	Ich finde es langweilig: es gibt nicht genug gute Sendungen. Ich gehe lieber aus.
Sieht deine Familie oft fern? (Again, say two things at least: you could include yourself in the answer as well.)	Meine Eltern sehen nicht viel fern, aber ich und meine Schwester sehen jeden Abend fern.
Wie findest du Seifenopern? (This allows a different tense.)	Als ich jünger war, habe ich sie gut gefunden. Jetzt finde ich, sie sind nicht so interessant.
Was siehst du gern? (A chance to say lots here, but no lists!)	Ich sehe gern Sport, und ich mag auch australische Seifenopern. Mein Lieblingsprogramm ist aber MTV.
Was magst du nicht? (Again, say lots, but don't use lists.)	Ich mag überhaupt nicht die Nachrichten, und Dokumentarfilme finde ich langweilig, so wie politische Sendungen.
Was ist deine Lieblingssendung? (Use the opportunity to justify an opinion.)	Meine Lieblingssendung ist „Die Simpsons", denn ich finde Bart sehr lustig.
Wie oft siehst du fern? (A chance to use a past tense.)	Ich habe viel ferngesehen, als ich jung war, aber jetzt nur dreimal die Woche.
Hast du gestern Abend ferngesehen? (Again, lots of potential, but don't use lists! Use opinions and different past tenses.)	Ich habe gestern einen alten Film, „The Matrix", gesehen: der Film war gut, und Keanu Reeves war fantastisch. Der Film hatte viele Effekte.

Grade-related criteria for speaking: conversation and role play

Although short conversations (of up to two minutes) may be the norm in performances at Foundation level, longer conversations should be the norm at General and Credit levels (up to a maximum of five minutes).

Chapter 10

SPEAKING

Foundation	General	Credit
The interlocutor: ◆ uses short phrases and sentences ◆ has to speak slowly, perhaps using repetition and/or rephrasing ◆ has to provide a great deal of (unsolicited) help	*The interlocutor:* ◆ goes beyond short phrases and sentences ◆ can usually speak at normal speed, using repetition and/or rephrasing as required ◆ has to provide some help	*The interlocutor:* ◆ can use a wide range of language ◆ can speak at normal speed, occasionally using repetition and/or rephrasing ◆ may have to provide minimal help
Candidates: ◆ can take part in simple conversations ◆ can ask for help, and with help provided can understand most of what is said ◆ tend to limit themselves to basic content and phrases ◆ may express simple opinions ◆ can make themselves understood ◆ beyond fixed phrases, the language tends to be inaccurate and hesitant, with mispronunciation, incorrect intonation, other-tongue interference and frequent grammatical errors ◆ have a limited range of vocabulary and structures	*Candidates:* ◆ can take part in simple conversations ◆ can understand most of what is said and can ask for help if required ◆ are prepared to go beyond basic content and phrases ◆ may take the initiative ◆ can express agreement, disagreement, opinions and reasons ◆ can communicate with some success and cope reasonably well with unexpected questions, although there may be many grammatical errors ◆ there may be mispronunciation, occasional other-tongue interference and weakness in intonation ◆ may speak carefully and deliberately with some accuracy or be more fluent but less accurate ◆ show a reasonable range of vocabulary and structures ◆ may attempt a range of tenses	*Candidates:* ◆ can take part in extended conversations ◆ can understand immediately almost everything said and seldom need to ask for help ◆ have no difficulty going beyond basic content and phrases ◆ readily take initiative ◆ express agreement, disagreement, opinions and reasons well and can expand on them if required ◆ have no difficulty making themselves understood and can use the language flexibly, coping well with unexpected questions ◆ are generally accurate although there may be occasional grammatical errors and weaknesses in pronunciation ◆ speak with little hesitation, other-tongue interference or weakness in intonation ◆ can use a range of language structures with some confidence ◆ may attempt a range of tenses

Grade 6	Grade 5	Grade 4	Grade 3	Grade 2	Grade 1
Interactions tend to be very limited in range. Candidates need a lot of unsolicited help.	Interactions are less limited in range and content. Candidates need some unsolicited help.	Interactions may be inaccurate with reasonable range, or more accurate but lacking in range.	Interactions are more accurate and vocabulary and structures are more wide-ranging.	Interactions are mostly accurate and candidate is able to use the language flexibly.	Candidates are able to converse at some length and show control of the language.

Chapter 10

The role play

This requires polite, formal language (the kind of language you might find in a transaction, a job interview and in a vocational situation). You must also use *Sie, Ihnen, Ihr,* and the verb forms that go with *Sie*. If it is a **transaction**, it will be fairly straightforward because the task will be structured, so you will know what you are expected to ask and can prepare this thoroughly. In a **vocational** situation, where the task will be more conversational, you should also follow the guidance given for the conversation type of assessment.

In this section, we will take you through preparing for both these types of assessment. However, remember that most of the advice in the conversation guidelines applies to this assessment as well, and make sure you have checked out the support on forming questions.

A transactional task

We will look at one kind of transactional task: however, the techniques and much of the advice here can be carried over to other tasks. This task is very straightforward, but it is one where the teacher might try to make things awkward, to allow you to 'negotiate', and deal with the unexpected.

Booking a hotel

You are intending to go to Germany with your family on holiday: you phone a hotel to try to book accommodation. Your teacher will play the part of the person at the hotel. Before you start, you should know how much you want to pay and what accommodation you are looking for!

You should carry out the following tasks:

- Ask if they have rooms available in July.
- Ask if they have rooms with a bath/shower.
- Ask if they have rooms with a balcony.
- Give some dates, and ask if the rooms are available then.
- Find out if there is a restaurant.
- Ask the cost for: (a) rooms (b) breakfast.
- Ask when breakfast will be served.
- Ask where exactly the hotel is.

Task	What you need to do
◆ Ask if they have rooms available in July.	Remember to start off by introducing yourself, and saying why you are calling: *Hallo, mein Name ist … Ich will eine Reservierung machen.* Be prepared to have to spell your name. You should also know how many rooms you want! *Haben Sie zwei Zimmer für …*
◆ Ask if they have rooms with a bath/shower.	Remember you must keep on using *Sie*, and remember to use the correct question form: *Haben Sie …?* You may be given an option in the answer, such as a price difference, and you should be ready for this: *Ich möchte lieber …*
◆ Ask if they have rooms with a balcony.	This gives you a chance to use a different tense, the conditional: *Haben Sie Zimmer mit Balkon?* or *Hätten Sie Zimmer mit Balkon?*
◆ Give some dates, and ask if the rooms are available then.	Try using the conditional here: *Wir möchten am … ankommen und bis zum … bleiben?* Again, be ready to accept different dates, if the teacher offers them, or to ask for an alternative: *Ja, das wäre möglich./Nein, das wäre nicht möglich … Könnten wir am … ankommen?*
◆ Find out if there is a restaurant.	Vary the way you ask questions: just use *es gibt* for this one: *Gibt es ein Restaurant?*
◆ Ask the cost for: (a) rooms (b) breakfast.	There are lots of ways of asking how much something costs: to vary it, you can just ask if breakfast is included: *Zwei Zimmer mit …, was kostet das? Ist Frühstück auch im Preis?* To make your conversation better, repeat the answer and write down the costs. And remember your budget: you might have to ask for cheaper rooms, if the prices you are quoted are too high: *Haben Sie Zimmer, die ein bisschen preiswerter sind?*
◆ Ask when breakfast will be served.	A straightforward question: *Um wie viel Uhr wird das Frühstück serviert?* To make your conversation better, repeat the answer and write down the times.
◆ Ask where exactly the hotel is.	A straightforward question, and a chance to note down the answer: *Wo genau liegt das Hotel?*
◆ And finally, remember to finish off the booking!	You could say you will write to confirm the booking: *Ich schreibe Ihnen, um die Reservierung zu konfirmieren.*

Chapter 10

A vocational role play

You have an interview for a job as a waiter in Germany for the summer. Your teacher will play the role of interviewer. This is a chance for you to give longer answers for a Credit grade, or more straightforward answers for a General grade. You should also use the chance to ask some questions. Some suggestions are added below, but make up more if you feel confident!

Questions	Some suggestions
Wie heißen Sie?	Remember to start of by saying hello! You could also add in your nationality and the answer to the next question: *Guten Tag. Ich heiße ..., und mein Vorname ist ... Ich bin Schotte/Schottin.*
Wie schreibt man das?	Know your alphabet!
Wie alt sind Sie?	You could also add in the answer to the next question: *Ich bin ... Jahre alt. Ich bin am ... geboren.*
Wann und wo sind Sie geboren?	Straightforward, if you know your numbers, and the chance to add your nationality, if you have not already done so: *Ich bin am vierzehnten November 1991 in Inverness in Schottland geboren.*
Wo wohnen Sie?	You can add the details about where you live, where exactly it is, and your address if you want: *Ich wohne in Dalkeith bei Edinburgh. Das liegt in Südostschottland. Meine Adresse ist ...*
Als was wollen Sie arbeiten?	You know the job, because it is in the instructions! You can add in the bit about your experience here, if you want to extend your answer: *Ich suche eine Arbeit als ... Ich war schon ... in Schottland.*
Haben Sie schon Erfahrung in diesem Gebiet?	A chance to give details, if you wish: where you worked, for how long, what you thought of it, and so on: *Ja, ich habe schon als ... bei ... gearbeitet. Ich war ... Jahre dort. Die Arbeit hat mir gefallen.*
Welche Sprachen kennen Sie?	Don't just give a list: say how you speak them, and how long you have been learning them: *Ich spreche fließend/sehr gut/ziemlich gut ... Ich lerne das seit ... Jahren.*

Questions	Some suggestions
Haben Sie jetzt eine Arbeit?	Another chance to give details, if you wish: where you work, how long you've been doing this, and so on: *Ja, ich arbeite seit ... bei ... Ich bin seit ... Jahren da. Ich mag gern meine Arbeit.*
Was können Sie über Sie selbst erzählen?	A chance to say nice things about yourself! *Ich bin fleißig, ehrlich, freundlich, und ich komme mit allen sehr gut aus!*
Wann könnten Sie anfangen?	A chance to answer the next question at the same time: *Ich könnte am ersten Juni anfangen.*
Wie lange wollen Sie bleiben?	*Ich möchte bis zum ersten September bleiben.*
Haben Sie Fragen zu der Arbeit?	A chance for you to ask some questions: *Kann ich im Hotel wohnen? Wie viele Stunden in der Woche werde ich arbeiten? Muss man viel am Wochenende arbeiten? Wie viel werde ich verdienen?*
	Remember to say goodbye properly! *Also danke und auf Wiedersehen.*

Chapter 11

WRITING

Writing is worth **one-sixth** of your overall Standard Grade result. You will have to carry out at least three writing assessments during your course, for a folio of work: the subjects of these pieces of writing will be set by your teacher in discussion with you, and you can draft and redraft following advice from your teacher. You can use textbooks and work you have already produced to guide you in your preparation, and you can work from guidelines provided by your teacher. This means you can really plan out what you want to write.

Your final pieces of writing must be done under controlled conditions, with only a dictionary and your memory to help you. You will have 30 minutes under exam conditions to produce each piece. The folio of three pieces will be sent to SQA for marking. However, you have a lot of control over what is in your folio, and you may have more than three pieces from which you and your teacher select the best. SQA will take the marks for your three tests and make an average of them: this will be your final writing grade.

The rules for the assessments are very open: you can write in a whole variety of different styles, and there are no kinds of writing you *must* do. You might find that the topics you are using for your speaking assessments will also do for your writing assessments, which could save you a lot of time and effort. Your writing will be graded according to how well it demonstrates a sense of structure, control of grammar, focus on the task and communication. The way of judging how well you have done is given in the grade-related criteria for writing: these are shown on page 83, so that you can see what is expected of you.

Grade-related criteria for writing

These criteria are to be understood as characteristics of writing at each level; thus, for example, the length of a piece of writing or its accuracy alone is not sufficient to guarantee an award at a particular level. The **overall quality** of the written language is what is being assessed.

Foundation	General	Credit
◆ the content is appropriate to the task, but very limited ◆ communication is achieved despite frequent grammatical errors ◆ candidates may express simple opinions ◆ candidates can use simple structures with some accuracy ◆ there is a limited range of vocabulary and structures ◆ there may be a tendency to repeat structures and/or phrases	◆ writing shows evidence of structure and/or focus ◆ communication is achieved with some success and consistency, despite grammatical errors ◆ candidates can express simple opinions and reasons ◆ candidates can use simple structures with more accuracy ◆ there is a reasonable range of vocabulary and structures ◆ there may be an attempt at a range of tenses	◆ writing is well structured and/or focused ◆ candidates can write with some flexibility ◆ candidates can express opinions and reasons well and may expand on them ◆ candidates are generally accurate in their use of language although there may be occasional grammatical errors, particularly in more complex structures ◆ there is evidence of a wide range of vocabulary and structures ◆ candidates use a range of tenses as appropriate

Grade 6	Grade 5	Grade 4	Grade 3	Grade 2	Grade 1
Writing is limited in range and very inaccurate.	Writing is limited in range, but may be more focused and/or accurate.	Writing may be inaccurate but with a reasonable range, or more accurate but lacking in range.	Writing is more accurate, and vocabulary and structures are more wide ranging.	Writing is mostly accurate but ideas are less well developed, or ideas are better developed but writing is less accurate.	Candidates are able to write at some length showing both development of ideas and control of the language.

For a Foundation award, about 25 words are needed in each piece. For a General award, you should be able to write 50 words or more. For a Credit award, you need 100 words or more for each piece. Normally you will need at least the minimum number of words to be able to show that you have a command of the structures and vocabulary necessary to demonstrate you are working at that level. However, what will be more important than the word count is your accuracy and sense of structure. We will look at how you can show this in the next pages.

For a Foundation award, it is important to write as accurately as you can! To get a General award, you will have to try to use a variety of tenses and structures. This means both past and present tenses, plus the use of some sub-clauses and auxiliaries like *kann, muss* and *möchte*. You should be able to give your opinions on what you are writing about, and you must try to be as accurate as you can. Your writing should always focus on the topic you have chosen.

For Credit, you will have to use more complex and sophisticated language. You must be reasonably accurate in your use of German, and use both past and present tenses well. Your opinions will be more important than at General level, and you should also include reasons for some of your opinions. Your writing will have to be more varied and flexible.

Planning your writing

Once you've chosen your topic area, focus on the actual language you will use. Try to look at two or three headings, to break the task down for you. Preparing a writing assessment is very like planning a prepared talk. The do's and don'ts are very similar.

Do's

- Do look at the textbook or texts you are working from for good ideas you can use.
- Do make sure you understand what you are writing, or it will be very difficult to remember it properly when you have to do the final writing for the folio.
- Do show a draft to your teacher, to get any suggestions, or so that you can make corrections.
- Do write on every second line, to make it easier to put in changes and corrections.
- Do use a variety of structures: use different tenses, use joining words like *weil* or *wenn* to make longer sentences, use adjectives, adverbs and phrases you know are correct. Remember that your word order is very important in showing you know about German structures!
- Do give your opinion, and work at using different ways to say what you think. Look at the section on giving opinions in Chapter 12.

Chapter 11

Don'ts

- Don't leave the preparation to the last minute! If you start your preparation early, you'll be able to ask your teacher for advice on any vocabulary or grammar you're unsure of.
- Don't always stick to safe, simple language. It may be easier, but it won't get the best grades. Try out some of the more impressive sentences you've learned. Note down useful vocabulary and phrases you've seen elsewhere under appropriate topic headings, so that you can reuse them in your writing assessments.
- Don't use lists of things, as these will not help you to show structure or knowledge of German. What will be more important than the actual number of words is the number and variety of structures.

To help you prepare for a writing assessment, we have selected three possible topics: one using **personal** language, one using **past tenses**, and the other using **discursive** language. We will guide you through the process involved in preparing for and carrying out the assessment: you can follow the same pattern for a topic of your own choice. You might also find Chapter 10 on speaking useful to help you prepare for a specific writing task.

1 A letter to a German-speaking friend
2 Meine Ferien
3 Freizeit

1 Personal language

A letter to a German-speaking friend

You decide to write a letter to a friend in German. Sort out your ideas and choose the areas you feel most confident about: best of all, the areas you have been covering in class recently. Think about ways of including different tenses and structures in your writing. Plan what you are going to write. We will imagine here that you are going to write about your family.

Look at the vocabulary in the vocabulary pages, and take what you think might help you. Look also at the structures suggested in Chapter 12, and take a few that you think will fit in with what you are going to say.

Now that you have chosen the kinds of things you are going to say, let us look at the first section. After beginning your letter with some letter-writing vocabulary, you are going to describe who is in your family. This lets you start off with simple language, which you should make sure is correct. You can use adjectives, and verbs with *er* and *sie*. You will also be able to use any special phrases you know, and you can introduce a couple of good structures to show that you know lots of good German! Here is an example of the kind of thing you could say:

> *Hallo Hans,*
> *wie geht's? Mir geht es gut. Du hast mir gebeten, etwas von meiner Familie zu erzählen. Also, es gibt bei uns meinen Vater Lewis, meine Mutter Yvonne, und meinen jungen Bruder Euan. Mein Vater ist 38 Jahre alt und hat kurze braune Haare. Yvonne, meine Mutter, ist klein und schlank.*

This is 50 words, and would be a start to producing a piece of writing at Credit level. If you add another couple of sentences, you will have a complete piece of writing at General level. For General, the following would fit the criteria:

> *Früher war mein Vater Soldat, jetzt arbeitet er bei der Post. Meine Mutter hat nie gearbeitet, denn sie hat uns Kinder! Wie sieht denn deine Familie aus?*

The second section for Credit level could go on to talk about how you get on with your parents: this paragraph can include a past tense, and allows you to give opinions. Here is an example of what you could write:

> *Ich komme mit meinem Vater gut aus, denn wir spielen beide sehr gern Fußball und sind auch große Fans von FC Aberdeen! Mit meiner Mutter habe ich mich immer sehr gut verstanden, denn sie hat mir bei meinen Hausaufgaben viel geholfen, als ich klein war und Probleme mit der Schularbeit hatte.*

This adds another 50 words to your writing, and shows a variety of tenses and structures. Finally, you could prepare a section on a problem you have, to get more variety in. This is the kind of thing you might write:

> *Das einzige Problem ist, dass ich in der Woche sehr früh zu Hause sein muss, während meine Freunde lange in der Stadt bleiben können. Das finde ich unfair. Wann musst du abends zu Hause sein?*
>
> *Ich muss jetzt gehen, also tschüs!*

These three paragraphs make up about 150 words, which is right for Credit level. They also give you a variety of structures. What you need to be able to do is understand what you have written so that you can remember it when you actually have to do the folio piece of writing. So follow the golden rules:

1. Make sure you choose work you are familiar with.
2. Make sure you know it's correct.
3. Use a variety of tenses and structures.
4. Do the proofreading when you have finished!

2 Past tenses

Meine Ferien

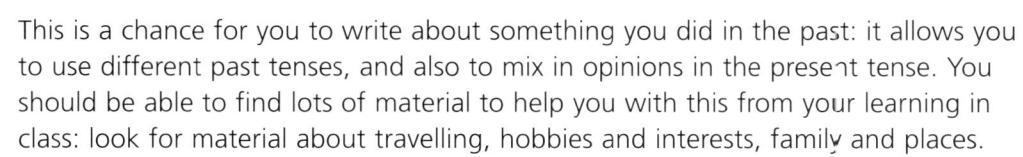

This is a chance for you to write about something you did in the past: it allows you to use different past tenses, and also to mix in opinions in the present tense. You should be able to find lots of material to help you with this from your learning in class: look for material about travelling, hobbies and interests, family and places.

Let us imagine you are going to describe a past holiday in Spain. The first section could describe who you went with, how you got there, and where you stayed. This would be a Foundation text, the first half of a General piece of writing, or the introduction to a Credit piece:

> *Letzten Sommer bin ich nach Spanien gefahren. Ich war mit meiner Familie, und wir sind von Glasgow nach Malaga geflogen. Wir waren zwei Wochen lang in einem Hotel am Strand. Das Wetter war fantastisch.*

The next section would be the final part of a General piece, or the second part of a Credit text. In this, you could talk about what you did there, and include an opinion:

> *Ich habe jeden Tag im Meer geschwommen und habe auch in der Sonne gelegen: ich war sehr braun! Ich habe Paella gegessen: das war ziemlich gut. Ich hatte viel Spaß abends in der Hoteldisko.*

To put this into the Credit category, you could add a final section about what other people did and thought. Try to include a variety of tenses and structures:

> *Meine Eltern hatten auch viel Spaß, mein Vater kriegte aber einen Sonnenbrand: er war total rot. Meine Mutter hat das lustig gefunden. Ich möchte nächstes Jahr wieder nach Spanien fliegen, weil das Wetter so warm und sonnig ist. Ich hoffe, dass wir das machen.*

3 Discursive writing

Freizeit

This style of writing will allow you to write about a topic using lots of opinion words and good phrases from the texts you are working from, so your first task should be to look at your source texts and select some phrases. Then, break your task into areas. For a Foundation award, you could write a section about what you do in your free time. For a General award, you could start with a section about what you do, then go on to talk about your favourite activity. For Credit, you could write a section about what you do, followed by a section about what other young people in your class do (allowing you to put in third person verbs), and then finish by writing about the dangers of too many passive hobbies and not enough exercise.

Chapter 11

The first section might read something like this:

In meiner Freizeit treibe ich viel Sport. Ich spiele gern Fußball und im Sommer spiele ich auch Tennis. Im Winter sehe ich fern: meine Lieblingssendung ist natürlich eine Sportsendung. Manchmal sehe ich gern Rugby am Wochenende. Ich gehe auch aus und treffe mit meinen Freunden. Das ist immer Spaß.

That gives you about 50 words, with some opinions and a variety of structures: most of the sentences have *ich* in them, but they start in different ways. You could take out some of the harder words to remember and make it about 40 words.

The second section could be either of these two:

(General) *Mein Lieblingssport ist aber Fußball. Ich habe in der Grundschule für die Schulmannschaft gespielt, und ich spiele jetzt mit meinen Freunden: ich finde das gut, denn es ist nicht zu stressig.*

This gives you a total of more than 70 words, and has a past tense in it as well as an opinion and a reason. You could also use this for Credit level, but add more to it:

(Credit) *Meine Freunde sind nicht alle so sportlich wie ich: früher waren sie sportlich, jetzt aber möchten sie lieber am Wochenende in die Stadt gehen. Das finde ich blöd, und ich möchte weiter fit bleiben.*

You have the chance to demonstrate a variety of tenses and verb structures here, and show that you have a good knowledge of more than the basics! In the final section, it is the chance to show ways of expressing opinions and giving reasons for your opinions:

Es ist wichtig, fit zu bleiben. Man kann besser leben, wenn man fit ist: ich möchte nicht später in fünf Jahren nicht mehr Fußball spielen, weil Sport treiben für mich sehr wichtig ist.

Once you have written your first draft, had it corrected, and have a good version which you are going to learn for the day of the actual assessment, how can you go about learning it? There are various things you can try:

1. First, if at all possible, produce your writing as a word-processed document: this makes it easier to change, draft and redraft. You can then take that document and make a new copy with every second word blanked out, to help you remember what you wrote the first time. You can then go to a version which only has a few key words left, as a guideline to writing out the text again.

2. You might find it helpful just to write out the document several times. Each time you do so, compare it carefully with the original, to make sure you are not putting in errors. This is called proofreading, and is an essential part of the task!

3. Get somebody to help you, if you can: they can hold the original text, and give you clue words when you need them, as you try to remember what you have written.

Finally, on the day of the assessment, remember that you are only allowed a dictionary and your memory. You will have 30 minutes to produce the writing, but you should not need all this time if you are prepared. You should not be using your dictionary at this stage to look up any new words, as this might introduce new errors! Instead, use it as you go along and after you have finished to check what you have written for accuracy. Remember also to look at your verb endings, as the accuracy of these will have a big influence on what grade you are awarded.

The most important factor in getting a good writing grade is preparation: make sure you research your first draft, have it corrected, and have your final working draft checked and correct. This all takes time, so make sure you start early!

Chapter 12

STRUCTURES AND VOCABULARY

To help you in both speaking and writing, this chapter should act as a reference when producing your own work. As you may see when you look at the grade-related criteria in Chapters 10 and 11, you will be assessed in both skills on your use of structure, your use of opinions and reasons, and your use of a variety of grammatical structures and tenses, as well as (of course) on the accuracy of your writing and speaking! You should try to make sure that your preparation for writing and speaking works towards these criteria.

Structure

This means that your work should be directly related to the topic you are writing or speaking about. You should not just collect a whole set of different phrases and sentences, and jumble them all together. Best of all is the structure where you introduce the topic, give your opinions, and come to a conclusion.

If you are talking about school, you should not include a whole lot of material about where you live, how old you are, and your family. This is irrelevant!

You should also avoid the temptation to give long lists: when talking about sport, for instance, do not simply give a list of sports you do, and when talking about television, avoid giving a list of your favourite programmes.

If you write a letter, start and finish it properly. Avoid starting every sentence in the same way, for example, *Ich ... Ich ...*

Giving opinions

Remember that the German way of saying 'I like' is often very different from English. 'I like playing' and 'I like going' become *Ich spiele gern* and *Ich gehe gern*. 'I like Edinburgh' and 'I like holidays' become *Mir gefällt Edinburgh* and *Mir gefallen die Ferien*. Remember the rules of word order when using these structures! You might also find the following phrases useful in giving your opinions:

Chapter 12

Ich esse so gern Schokolade.	I really like chocolate.
Ich sehe echt gern Seifenopern.	I really like watching soaps.
Ich mache nicht sehr gern Hausaufgaben.	I don't really like doing homework.
Ich spiele lieber Tennis.	I prefer playing tennis.
Ich mag gern Fußball.	I like football.
Ich mag nicht …	I don't like …
Ich hasse …	I hate …
Ich kann … nicht ausstehen.	I really hate …
Ich glaube, es ist …	I think it's …
Ich finde das toll.	I find that terrific.
Ich finde es doof, dass …	I find it stupid that …
Es ist fantastisch, super, sehr gut, interessant, aufregend, lustig, schrecklich, traurig, deprimierend, Quatsch, langweilig.	It's fantastic, great, very good, interesting, exciting, fun, awful, sad, depressing, nonsense, boring.
Es ist besser/schlechter, … zu …	It is better/worse to …
Es ist besser, auf dem Land zu wohnen.	It is better to live in the country.
Es gibt/Es gab zu viel/viele …	There is/There were too much/many …
Es gibt nicht genug …	There is not enough …
Es wäre gut, wenn …	It would be good if …
Meiner Meinung nach …	In my opinion …
Man muss wissen, dass …	You have to know that …
Man darf nicht vergessen, dass…	We mustn't forget that …
Wir sollen … Wir sollen nicht …	We should/shouldn't …
Ich möchte wissen, ob …	I would like to know whether …
Ich möchte sehen, dass …	I would like to see that …

STRUCTURES AND VOCABULARY

Chapter 12

Giving reasons

Giving reasons for your opinions, or for why things happen, can be done by using conjunctions. It is a good idea to do this, as it allows you to achieve two things at the same time: you are expressing yourself, and you are also using more complex structures and language. Conjunctions, or joining words, are words like *weil, denn, wenn* and *da,* which say why something is the way it is. Remember that many conjunctions in German will send the verb to the end of the clause or sentence. (Exceptions are *und, aber, oder, denn* and *sondern*.) You will find a quick guide to word order on page 95.

Look at the sentences below to see some conjunctions in action when discussing pocket money, giving an opinion followed by a reason. Try to use at least two sentences like this in every piece of writing you do, and make sure you leave an opportunity for sentences like this in your preparation for speaking assessments.

Ich habe nie genug Taschengeld, denn ich kaufe mir zu viel Klamotten.	I never have enough pocket money, since I buy too many clothes.
Meine Mutter gibt mir £10, wenn ich im Hause helfe.	My mother gives me £10, if I help in the house.
Ich bekomme nicht viel Taschengeld, ich muss also samstags arbeiten.	I don't get a lot of pocket money, so I have to work on Saturdays.
Da ich arbeite, habe ich mehr Geld als meine Freunde.	Since I work, I have more money than my friends.
Weil ich für mein Geld arbeite, habe ich mehr Freiheit.	Because I work for my money, I have more freedom.

Grammatical variety

The marks you get for your speaking and writing assessments will be affected by the structures you use. Sometimes this means using good phrases and sentences you know, but often it is just a question of making sure all your sentences do not start with *ich*. Make sure you create opportunities to use *wir* and *man* (remembering to get the verb ending right). Try to use some sentences in which you talk about what other people think or do. Here is a list of things you might consider:

- Use adjectives with nouns, with the correct endings, of course: *Perth ist eine **ruhige** Stadt.*
- Use verbs of two words, putting the two words in the correct place: *Ich **gehe** oft in Glasgow **einkaufen**. Ich **bin** nach Aberdeen **gefahren**.*

- Use pronouns in your sentences: *Mein Bruder,* **er** *ist sechs Jahre alt. Ich finde* **ihn** *nervend.*
- Use modal verbs:

Ich **muss** … gehen.	I have to go …
Du **sollst** wissen, dass …	You should know that …
Man **kann** viel bei uns unternehmen.	There's lots to do where we are.

Tenses

Another thing to think about is the use of a variety of tenses. Every speaking or writing task should use at least two different tenses. This means planning the tenses when you do your preparation. If you are discussing school, for instance, you could say what things used to be like, what will happen next year, and what you would like to happen. If you are discussing clothes, again you can say what you or other people used to wear, and what you are intending to buy this weekend! German makes this easy for us by only using a very small number of tenses. If you are unsure about tenses, look at the section on verbs on page 98.

For the purpose of preparing for Standard Grade assessments, we can divide the tenses into three areas: present, past and future. Let us look at each of these three areas.

The present

The present tense only has one form, but you can expand on this by using modal verbs or auxiliaries. Here are some examples of this:

Ich will am Wochenende arbeiten.	I want to work at the weekend.
Man kann nicht viel bei uns unternehmen.	You can't do a lot where we live.
Man muss nach Glasgow gehen, um einen Film zu sehen.	You have to go to Glasgow to see a film.
Ich muss viel zu Hause machen.	I have to do a lot at home.

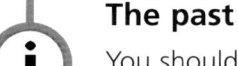

The past

You should be able to use two tenses in the past: these tenses have various names, although most books refer to them as the perfect and the preterite. You should use the perfect with most verbs, and the preterite of *sein*, *haben* and the six modal verbs (*dürfen, können, mögen, müssen, sollen, wollen*). If most of what you are discussing is in the present, then put in one or both of these tenses as well!

Chapter 12

Remember that the perfect always has two words, and to think about their place in the sentence. The auxiliary normally comes second, and the past participle comes last.

Here are some examples of the kind of thing you might say using the **perfect** tense, when discussing your hobbies:

Ich habe früher Fußball gespielt.	I used to play football.
Ich bin oft ins Schwimmbad gegangen.	I often went to the pool.
Wir haben letzten Samstag gewonnen.	We won last Saturday.
Ich habe Deutschland nie besucht.	I have never been to Germany.

Here are some examples of the **preterite** tense:

Ich war nie in Deutschland.	I have never been to Germany.
Ich hatte viel Spaß beim Spiel.	I had a lot of fun at the game.
Ich konnte gut schwimmen.	I was able to swim well.
Ich musste früh aufstehen.	I had to get up early.

The future

The normal way to talk about the future in German is very straightforward. You just use the present tense, along with a word or phrase like *morgen* or *nächste Woche*:

Morgen fahre ich nach Perth.	I'm going to Perth tomorrow.
Ich besuche nächste Woche meine Tante.	I'll visit my aunt next week.

However, you should also use the **formal future** and the **conditional** now and then, to show what a master of German tenses you are! Below, you will find some examples of this, with sentences referring to your plans for the future.

The formal future

This tense is very simple to use, but you have to remember your word order rules: the verb has two words, and they will normally come second and last in the sentence.

Ich werde in zwei Wochen da sein.	I'll be there in two weeks' time.
Nächstes Jahr werde ich die Abitur machen.	I'll do my Highers next year.
Ich werde auf die Uni gehen.	I shall go to university.
Meine Freundin wird nach Aberdeen gehen.	My friend is going to go to Aberdeen.

The conditional

This is also very easy to use, as it normally involves using only the infinitive of any verb, along with an auxiliary. There are some very straightforward phrases using the conditional which would fit most pieces of writing. It talks about what *could* happen. Here are four examples, used to talk about your plans for the summer:

Ich **möchte** nach Spanien **fahren**.	I'd like to go to Spain.
Ich **würde** gern mit meinen Freunden **fahren**.	I'd like to go with my friends.
Ich **würde** nicht in den Ferien **arbeiten**.	I wouldn't work during the holidays.
Es **wäre** fantastisch, wenn ich genug Geld **hätte**.	It would be great if I had enough money.

Word order

Word order is very important in German, and we can find it difficult because the rules are so different from English and do not seem logical to us. However, only a few of them are important at Standard Grade level, so let us look at what they are:

1 The verb comes second in a sentence.
2 A verb of two words comes second and last.
3 In a sub-clause, the verb goes to the end.
4 Adverbs and adverb phrases come in the order time – manner – place.

1 The verb comes second

This means that the verb is the second 'idea' (not the second 'word') in a sentence. You could begin the sentence with the subject: *Ich*, or *Mein kleiner Bruder*; or you might start with the object: *Meine Schule*. You could also start off with *Gestern* or *Letzte Woche*. You might even start off with a whole sub-clause: *Als ich zwölf Jahre alt war*. In each of these cases, the verb has to come next:

Chapter 12

> Mein kleiner Bruder **ist** sehr ärgerlich.
>
> Meine Schule **finde** ich gut.
>
> Letzte Woche **war** ich in Glasgow.
>
> Als ich zwölf Jahre alt war, **war** ich sehr sportlich.

2 Second and last

In past tense phrases (like *ich bin gegangen* or *ich habe gesehen*) and auxiliary verb phrases (like *meine Schwester kann essen*), the verb consists of two words. These two words come second and last in a sentence:

> Ich **bin** in die Stadt **gegangen**.
>
> Ich **habe** einen guten Film **gesehen**.
>
> Meine Schwester **kann** kein Fleisch **essen**.

3 In a sub-clause

In a sub-clause, the part of the verb which changes its endings (the auxiliary verb) will move from second to the very end.

> Ich kam spät, weil ich in die Stadt **gegangen bin**.
>
> Ich bin froh, wenn ich einen guten Film **gesehen habe**.
>
> Ich finde es doof, dass meine Schwester kein Fleisch **essen kann**.
>
> Als ich zwölf Jahre alt **war**, war ich sehr sportlich.

4 Time – manner – place

In German, we must always use the order 'when, how, where'. English normally says 'where' before 'when'.

> Ich gehe morgen mit dem Bus in die Stadt.   *I'm going to town tomorrow by bus.*

(!) Remember these four rules in your writing, and the examiner will be able to say that you show 'control in more complex structures'.

Subjects and objects: cases

Whether we call them subject and object, or nominative and accusative, not to mention dative, this is the most difficult thing for us to grasp when we are at the early stages of learning German. What are cases? These are words we use to describe the role of a noun in a sentence. The role of the noun depends upon two things: whether it is organised by a verb or a preposition.

Noun organised by a verb

To understand how this works, we must first go back to the verb: the verb is very important in any sentence, and in fact any group of words without a verb is not a sentence. So to understand subject and object, you first have to be able to identify the verb or verbs. This is made easier by knowing where to look for them: remember they are always second idea or last in a sentence.

Once you have found the verb, the **subject** (**nominative**) is the person or thing which is **doing**:

Mein kleiner Bruder ist sehr ärgerlich.	**My little brother** is annoying.
Meine Schule finde **ich** gut.	**I** find my school good.
Ich habe einen guten Film gesehen.	**I** saw a good film.

The **object** (**accusative**) (and very often there will not be one) is the person or thing having the action of the verb **done** to them:

Mein kleiner Bruder mag nicht **Gemüse**.	My little brother doesn't like **vegetables**.
Meine Schule finde ich gut.	I find **my school** good.
Ich habe **einen guten Film** gesehen.	I saw **a good film**.

The **indirect object** (**dative**) does not feature in every sentence. It is the person or thing something is **done to**:

Ich habe **meinem Bruder** mein Fahrrad geliehen.	I lent my bike **to my brother**.

You will find tables of endings in books, dictionaries and probably in your own exercise books! Don't be afraid to refer to them, but remember the rules above when you are using them. Get these endings right, and your written work in particular will seem so much better.

Chapter 12

Noun organised by a preposition

We have looked at verbs, and now for prepositions. A preposition is a word like 'in' or 'on', which might tell you where something is. These words often change the German for 'the', to make it **accusative** or **dative**: *der* Bruder, *für* **den** Bruder, *mit* **dem** Bruder. The same happens with words like *mein, ein, kein*: **mein** Bruder, *für* **meinen** Bruder, *mit* **meinem** Bruder.

The tables below show the pattern:

	masculine	feminine	neuter	plural
subject (nominative)	der	die	das	die
object (accusative)	den	die	das	die
indirect object (dative)	dem	der	dem	den

	masculine	feminine	neuter	plural
subject (nominative)	mein	meine	mein	meine
object (accusative)	meinen	meine	mein	meine
indirect object (dative)	meinem	meiner	meinem	meinen

Verbs

What is a verb? You will remember from primary that it is a 'doing word', but this definition is not good enough to let you work between English and German. First, we could say that a verb is a 'doing, being, having' word: this lets us see that words like 'am', 'is' and 'have' are verbs as well. Then we must remember that auxiliaries are verbs as well: 'can', 'must', 'should' and so on. We also need to know that in German a verb will often be made up of two words: *bin gegangen, habe gesehen, kann gehen*.

English has a large number of tenses, with some of them using three or four words to make up a verb: 'I have been going', for instance. Normal conversational German or informal letter writing uses a much smaller number of tenses: see page 93 for the ones you need to know for Standard Grade. Remember not to make the mistake of trying to translate every word in an English verb: 'I am going' becomes *ich gehe*, 'I have been seeing' becomes *ich sehe*.

The following table is something you should know and understand:

Chapter 12

person	singular	plural
1st	ich (*I*)	wir (*we*)
2nd	du (*you*) (*informal, for one person*) Sie (*you*) (*formal*)	ihr (*you*) (*informal, for more than one person*) Sie (*you*) (*formal*)
3rd	er (*he*) sie (*she*) es (*it*)	sie (*they*)

Make sure you can take any German verb you know, and put it into the table above with the correct endings on. If you can't do this, you need to practise! Here are four important verbs to start you off:

gehen

person	singular	plural
1st	ich gehe	wir gehen
2nd	du gehst Sie gehen	ihr geht Sie gehen
3rd	er geht sie geht es geht	sie gehen

sein

person	singular	plural
1st	ich bin	wir sind
2nd	du bist Sie sind	ihr seid Sie sind
3rd	er ist sie ist es ist	sie sind

haben

person	singular	plural
1st	ich habe	wir haben
2nd	du hast Sie haben	ihr habt Sie haben
3rd	er hat sie hat es hat	sie haben

Chapter 12

können

person	singular	plural
1st	ich kann	wir können
2nd	du kannst Sie können	ihr könnt Sie können
3rd	er kann sie kann es kann	sie können

Use this blank table as a template: see if you can fit in every verb you know.

person	singular	plural
1st	ich	wir
2nd	du Sie	ihr Sie
3rd	er sie es	sie

Use exactly the same table structure for putting in your past tense forms. There are two different ways this might work:

person	singular	plural
1st	ich hatte	wir hatten
2nd	du hattest Sie hatten	ihr hattet Sie hatten
3rd	er hatte sie hatte es hatte	sie hatten

person	singular	plural
1st	ich war	wir waren
2nd	du warst Sie waren	ihr wart Sie waren
3rd	er war sie war es war	sie waren

The verb list in your dictionary will tell you which form goes into the *ich* box: this will help you to work out the rest.

Chapter 12

Vocabulary

These pages are for your reference. When you are getting ready for a listening or reading test, you should check that you know the vocabulary in each topic area, and you can use the pages as a revision guide. When you have a writing or speaking task, use the vocabulary to help you with ideas. Each section has some starter sentences, but there is also space for you to add your own sentences and phrases: things that you know are correct and that you think will fit the task. Whenever you see a good phrase, just note it down and then write it in the space provided in each topic area. Check the gender and the plural form, if you need these, and remember that the capitals are very important – they count as spelling.

These are the areas covered:

1 Using numbers (including times, dates, temperatures, distances and prices)
2 Days, months, weeks and years
3 Jobs and professions
4 School, including subjects studied
5 Food and drink
6 Family members
7 The weather and seasons
8 Hobbies and sports
9 House, daily routine and household tasks
10 Places in town
11 Modes of transport

1 Using numbers

Times

neun Uhr	nine o'clock
zehn nach neun	ten past nine
Viertel nach neun	quarter past nine
halb **zehn**	half past nine (remember it is half **to** the hour)
Viertel vor neun	quarter to nine
zehn vor neun	ten to nine

Chapter 12

Remember that most official times in German will use the 24-hour clock, and there is no use of 'am' or 'pm'.

dreizehn Uhr	one pm
achtzehn Uhr dreißig	6.30 pm

Dates

Mittwoch, der 25. November	Wednesday the 25th of November
Ich bin am 14. Oktober geboren	I was born on October 14th

Temperatures

Germany, like most other countries in the world, uses centigrade to measure temperatures. So a weather forecast will say something like, *'Heute ist es fünfzehn Grad'*. Make sure you know your numbers!

Distances

Remember that you should never use measurements like miles when talking and writing in German, but always metres and kilometres:

Glasgow liegt 80 Kilometer westlich von Edinburgh.

Ich wohne 500 Meter von der Schule.

Prices

Prices are all in Euros and cents. (Old prices in DM are still in some books, but they will not feature in your exam.)

When writing about yourself, you should use 'Pfund' for pounds:

Ich verdiene zehn Pfund die Woche.

Put your own phrases in the spaces below:

2 Days, weeks, months and years

Montag	Monday
Dienstag	Tuesday
Mittwoch	Wednesday
Donnerstag	Thursday
Freitag	Friday
Samstag	Saturday
Sonntag	Sunday
Januar	January
Februar	February
März	March
April	April
Mai	May
Juni	June
Juli	July
August	August
September	September
Oktober	October
November	November
Dezember	December
der Vormittag, der Morgen	morning
vormittags	in the morning
der Nachmittag	afternoon
der Abend	evening (until about 11pm)
abends	in the evening, at night
die Nacht	night (after 11pm or m dnight)

Chapter 12

heute abend	tonight
gestern	yesterday
vorgestern	the day before yesterday
morgen	tomorrow
übermorgen	the day after tomorrow
montags	on Mondays
eine Woche	a week
vierzehn Tage	a fortnight
ein Monat	a month
ein Jahr	a year
Ich bin 15 Jahre alt	I am 15

Put your own phrases in the spaces below:

3 Jobs and professions

Remember that when saying what someone does for a living, you don't need ein/der. For example: *mein Vater ist Verkäufer* (my father is a shop assistant). Also remember that, if you are talking about a woman, you shoud add *–in* to most words, such as **Polizist/Polizistin**. Where this is not the case, both male and female forms are given.

Chapter 12

Arzt/Ärztin	doctor
Arbeitsloser/Arbeitslose	unemployed person
Bäcker	baker
Bauarbeiter	bricklayer, builder
Bauer/Bäuerin	farmer
Chef	boss or owner
Coiffeur	hairdresser
Direktor	managing director
Elektriker	electrician
Gärtner	gardener
Ingenieur	engineer
Journalist	journalist
Kassierer	cashier
Kellner	waiter/waitress
Klempner	plumber
Koch/Köchin	cook
Krankenpfleger	nurse
Lehrer	teacher
Mechaniker	mechanic
Metzger	butcher
Polizist	policeman
Postbeamter/ Postbeamte	postie
Schauspieler	actor
Schuldirektor	headteacher or director
Sekretär	secretary
Steward/Stewardess	air steward, air hostess
Taxifahrer	taxi driver
Techniker	technician
Verkäufer	shop assistant
Zahnarzt/ Zahnärztin	dentist

STRUCTURES AND VOCABULARY

Chapter 12

Starter sentences

Meine Mutter ist Lehrerin	My mum is a teacher
Ich möchte Krankenpflegerin werden	I'd like to be a nurse
Ich gehe auf die Uni	I'm going to go to university
Ich bleibe auf der Schule/in der Schule	I'm going to stay on at school
Ich arbeite samstags in einem Geschäft	I work in a shop on Saturdays
Ich trage Zeitungen aus	I deliver newspapers

Put your own phrases in the spaces below:

4 School subjects

Biologie	biology
Bürostudien	business management
Chemie	chemistry
Deutsch	German
Englisch	English
Erdkunde	geography
Französisch	French
Geschichte	history
Hauswirtschaft	home economics
Informatik	IT

Kunst	art
Mathe	maths
Musik	music
Naturwissenschaften	science
Physik	physics
Politik	modern studies
Sport	PE
Spanisch	Spanish
Technologie	technological studies
Werken	craft and design

School (general)

das Abitur	equivalent to Highers
die Bibliothek	library
ein Fach	a subject
mein Lieblingsfach/meine Lieblingsfächer	my favourite subject(s)
die Ferien	holidays
die Sommerferien	summer holidays
die Osterferien, die Weihnachtsferien	Easter, Xmas holidays
Hausaufgaben	homework
die Kantine	canteen
die Klassenarbeit	class test
das Klassenzimmer	classroom
die Note (gute Noten)	mark (good marks)
die Pause	break
eine Prüfung	exam
Schüler/ Schülerin	pupil
eine Stunde	lesson (also means an hour!)
die Uni/Universität	uni/university
das Zeugnis	report

Chapter 12

Useful school adjectives

aufregend	exciting, great
blöd	stupid
fantastisch, toll	great
gut (ich bin gut in)	good at
interessant	interesting
langweilig	boring
leicht	easy
lustig	funny
nützlich	useful
schwach (ich bin schwach in)	not so good at
schwer	hard
schwierig	difficult
streng	strict

Remember, when writing about school, do **not** give long lists of subjects you take!

Starter sentences

Ich mache meine Prüfungen im Mai	I'm going to sit my exams in May.
Ich hoffe, ich bekomme gute Noten	I hope to pass my exams
Ich habe gute Noten in…	I got good marks in…
Meine Lieblingsfächer sind…	My favourite subjects are…
Was ich gar nicht leiden kann, ist…	What I really don't like is…
Ich denke, der Lehrer ist schrecklich	I think that the teacher is awful
Ich meine, ich kriege zu viele Hausafgaben	I have too much homework, I think
Nächstes Jahr bleibe ich auf der Schule	I'm staying on next year

Put your own phrases in the spaces below:

5 Food and drink

der Apfel	an apple
eine Banane	banana
Bonbons/Süßigkeiten	sweets
ein Brot	(a loaf of) bread
ein Brötchen	a roll
Butter	butter
ein Ei	egg
Gemüse	vegetables
ein Jogurt	yoghurt
Kartoffelchips	crisps
Kartoffeln	potatoes
Käse	cheese
die Marmelade	jam
Nudeln	pasta
Obst	fruit
Pommes	chips
Rosenkohl	Brussels sprouts

Chapter 12

Sahne	cream
Schinken	ham
die Schokolade	chocolate
eine Tomate	tomato
die Wurst	sausage
ein Kaffee	coffee
eine Cola/Kola	coke
eine Limo	lemonade
Milch	milk
Mineralwasser	mineral water
Orangensaft	orange juice
Tee	tea
Wasser	water
Wein	wine

Starter sentences

Mein Lieblingsgericht ist…	My favourite food is…
Ich trinke sehr gern Tee	I love tea
Ich esse gern Obst	I like fruit a lot
Ich mag Pommes	I like chips
Ich trinke nicht gern Kaffee	I don't really like coffee
Salat kann ich nicht leiden	I hate salad
Nachmittags habe ich oft Hunger	I'm often hungry in the afternoons

Put your own phrases in the spaces below:

6 Family members

die Familie	family
die Eltern	parents
der Vater	father
die Mutter	mother
der Mann	husband
die Frau	wife
der Bruder, mein älterer Bruder	brother, my older brother
die Schwester, meine jüngere Schwester	sister, my younger sister
Stiefbruder/Stiefschwester	step brother/sister
der Sohn	son
die Tochter	daughter
Zwillingsbruder/Zwillingsschwester	twin
der Großvater/Opa	grandfather
die Großmutter/Oma	grandmother
der Enkel, die Enkelin	grandson/granddaughter
der Onkel	uncle
die Tante	aunt
der Vetter/der Kusin, die Kusine	cousin
der Neffe	nephew
die Nichte	niece

Chapter 12

Starter sentences

Wir sind vier in der Familie	There are four of us
Ich habe keine Geschwister	I don't have any brothers/sisters
Ich habe einen Bruder und zwei Schwestern	I have a sister and two brothers
Mein Bruder/meine Schwester heißt … .	My brother/sister is called….
Meine Eltern heißen…	My parents are called….
Meine Eltern sind getrennt/geschieden	My parents are separated/divorced
Ich komme mit meinen Eltern gut aus	I get on well with my parents
Meine Eltern sind echt nett	My parents are very nice
Manchmal streite ich mich mit meiner Mutter	I sometimes have arguments with mum
Meine Schwester ist richtig süß	My sister is very sweet
Ich kann mit…über meine Probleme sprechen	I can speak about my problems with…
Mit meinem Bruder verstehe ich mich nicht	I don't get on well with my brother
Mein Bruder nervt mich	My brother gets on my nerves

Put your own phrases in the spaces below:

7 The weather

ein Wetterbericht	weather forecast
Wie ist das Wetter?	What is the weather like?
Es ist jeden Tag schön	The weather is nice every day
Es ist ab und zu sonnig	It is sunny now and then
Es ist warm (Es ist nie warm)	It is hot (It's never hot)
Es sind 25°	It is 25° centigrade
Das Wetter ist oft mies	The weather is often bad
Im Winter ist es meistens kalt	It is usually cold in winter
Nachts friert es	It freezes at night
Es ist ziemlich oft windig	It is quite often windy
Im Herbst ist es neblig	It is foggy in autumn
Jetzt regnet es	It is raining now
Im Winter schneit es	It snows in winter

Seasons

der Frühling	spring
der Sommer	summer
der Herbst	autumn
der Winter	winter

Put your own phrases in the spaces below:

Chapter 12

8 Hobbies and sports

ich gehe ins Kino	I go to the cinema
ich gehe angeln	I go fishing
ich höre Musik	I listen to music
ich lese Zeitschriften/Bücher	I read magazines/books
ich sehe fern/ich schaue DVDs	I watch TV/DVDs
ich gehe Schlittschuh laufen	I go ice-skating
ich fahre Rad	I go on my bike
ich fahre Mountainbike	I go mountain biking
ich gehe skateboarden	I go boarding
ich reite	I go horse-riding
ich turne	I do gymnastics
ich gehe schwimmen	I go swimming
ich fahre Ski	I go skiing
ich treibe Sport	I do sport
ich segle	I go sailing
ich spiele Videospiele	I play video games.
ich spiele mit dem Computer	I play on the computer.
ich spiele Gitarre/Geige	I play the guitar/the violin
ich spiele Fußball, Rugby, Hockey	I play…

Starter sentences

In Glasgow gibt es viel zu tun	There is lots to do in Glasgow.
Es gibt nichts für junge Leute	There is nothing for young people.
Hier ist nicht viel los	There is not a lot here.
Es gibt kein Kino	There is no cinema
Man kann ins Jugendzentrum gehen	You can go to the youth club

Chapter 12

Ich spiele jedes Wochenende Tennis	I play tennis every weekend
Ich gehe mit meinen Freunden ins Kino	I go to the cinema with my friends
Mein Lieblingssport ist…	My favourite sport is..
Ich spiele unheimlich gern Tennis	I really love playing tennis
Was ich überhaupt nicht leiden kann, ist…	What I really can't stand is…
Dienstags spiele ich Hockey: toll!	I play hockey on Tuesdays: brilliant!
Ich bin Mitglied in einem Golfverein	I'm in a golf club
Ich spiele in der Hockeymannschaft	I'm in the hockey team

Put your own phrases in the spaces below:

9 House, daily routine and household tasks

eine Wohnung	flat
das Haus	house
das Reihenhaus	terraced house
das Doppelhaus	semi-detached house
der Stock (im ersten, zweiten)	floor (first, second and so on)
das Erdgeschoss	ground floor
der Dachboden	attic
der Wohnblock	block of flats
das Esszimmer	dining room

STRUCTURES AND VOCABULARY

Chapter 12

das Badezimmer	bathroom
das Wohnzimmer	living room
der Keller	cellar
das Schlafzimmer	bedroom
die Küche	kitchen
die Waschküche	utility room
die Dusche	shower
ich stehe um… Uhr auf	I get up at…
ich wasche mich	I get washed
ich ziehe mich an	I get dressed
ich frühstücke	I have my breakfast
ich verlasse das Haus	I leave the house
ich fahre mit dem Bus	I get the bus
ich komme nach Hause	I get home
ich gehe ins Bett	I go to bed
ich gehe einkaufen	I do the shopping
ich helfe meiner Mutter	I help my mum
ich passe auf meinen kleinen Bruder auf	I look after my brother
ich koche	I do the cooking
ich mache das Abendessen	I make the tea.
ich arbeite im Garten	I work in the garden
ich mache mein Bett	I make my bed
ich spüle ab	I do the washing-up
ich trockne ab	I dry the dishes
ich wasche das Auto	I wash the car
ich decke den Tisch	I set the table
ich räume den Tisch ab	I clear the table
ich räume mein Zimmer auf	I tidy my room

Chapter 12

Starter sentences

Oft muss ich für Mutti einkaufen	I often do the messages for mum
Manchmal muss ich mein Zimmer putzen	Sometimes I have to clean my room.
Jeden Tag mache ich mein Bett : so doof ! :	I make my bed everyday: how boring !
Ich mache nie die Wäsche	I never do the washing

Put your own phrases in the spaces below:

10 Places in town

der Bahnhof	station
der Busbahnhof	bus station
die Bank/die Sparkasse	bank
die Bibliothek	library
die Brücke	bridge
die Bushaltestelle	bus stop
der Campingplatz	campsite
das Einkaufszentrum	shopping centre
die Eisbahn	skating rink
das Freibad	outdoor swimming pool

Chapter 12

der Flughafen	airport
die Fußgängerzone	pedestrian precinct
das Gebäude	building
das Geschäft/der Laden	shop
das Hallenbad	swimming pool
der Hafen	harbour, port
das Jugendzentrum	youth club
das Kaufhaus	department store
das Kino	cinema
die Kirche	church
das Krankenhaus	hospital
der Markt	market
das Museum	museum
das Parkhaus	multi-story car park
der Platz	square
die Post	post office
das Rathaus	town hall
das Schloss	castle
die Schule	school
die Sehenswürdigkeit	tourist sight
das Sportszentrum	sports complex
die Stadthalle	town hall (for concerts etc)
das Stadion	stadium
die Tankstelle	petrol station
das Theater	theatre
die U-Bahn-Station	underground station
das Verkehrsamt	tourist information

Starter sentences

In Perth gibt es viel zu tun und zu sehen!	There's a lot to do and see in Perth
Für junge Leute ist nicht viel los	There's not a lot for young people
Wir haben ein Hallenbad	We have a swimming pool
Wir haben keinen Bahnhof	We don't have a station
Ich wohne seit zwölf Jahren in Dumfries	I've lived in Dumfries for twelve years

Put your own phrases in the spaces below:

11 Modes of transport

mit dem Auto/mit dem Wagen	by car
mit dem Bus	by bus
mit dem Flugzeug	by plane
mit der Fähre/mit dem Boot/mit dem Schiff	by boat
mit der U-Bahn	by underground
mit der Strassenbahn	by tram
mit dem Mofa	by moped
zu Fuß	on foot
mit der Bahn/mit dem Zug	by train
mit dem Rad/mit dem Fahrrad	by bike

Chapter 12

Starter sentences

Meistens gehe ich zu Fuß in die Schule	Usually I walk to school
Wenn es regnet, nehme ich den Bus	I go by bus when it's raining
Ich fahre lieber mit dem Auto, denn es ist schneller	I prefer going by car, it's quicker
Wir sind mit der Bahn nach Deutschland gefahren	We went to Germany by train
Ich fahre lieber mit dem Rad, denn es ist einfacher	I prefer to go by bike, it's easier

Put your own phrases in the spaces below: